A fascinating read on how a heart-centric approach to business is becoming the norm in the post-COVID age. Learn how to connect to the hearts of your team members and customers to drive revenue and create a company culture that ensures lasting growth.

Lt General USMC (Ret.) Willie Williams

Succeed the Right Way is a brilliant example of the benefits of applying those basic maxims we all learned in childhood to our business practice. Learn to be the kind of mentor you wish you had when you were coming up in the business world!

Mathews Tembo | CEO and Founder,
Matt Children's Hope Foundation

Paul Gunn uses his own experiences to illustrate the necessity of channeling personal misfortunes into future growth. His personal story is as compelling as the guidance he offers. This is truly a remarkable read!

Matt Casto | President, THE Sports Agency

Paul Gunn, Jr. is a man of intention, value, leadership and his words in *Succeed the Right Way* speak to the true heart of the human being, the leader, the entrepreneur, the business owner, the change maker, the doer and the person with the talent and heart looking to make a big difference in this world.

I have read a lot of books in my lifetime but Paul's words navigate you through becoming an even better version of yourself through the practice of empathy. In a world where everyone is striving for greatness and the next opportunity, the fundamentals of this book will act as a reminder to "succeed the right way." It walks us through the powerful importance of the "domino effect" and impact we can have on others through our words, thinking and actions.

In a fast moving world his book will make you stand still and reflect on what it takes to build an empire from a place of compassion, drive, and vision. His honor, experience in running and building a successful company himself are evident in every avenue of this book. All I can say is that I feel blessed I crossed paths with this incredible thought leader. I wish Paul the best in all of his endeavours and I know that this is the first of many books we will see from him as he builds out his legacy. He is a true heart-centred leader. A change maker.

Justine Pogroske | Founder and Director of Million Dollar Branders

People always come first in business, and Paul Gunn reveals the secret to connecting organically with team members and customers in a way that ensures lasting and scalable growth. This is truly a masterclass.

Nicky Dare | Founder iDARE® Inc. and DARE Education, Educator and Bestselling Author of *Pandemic Survival & The Audacity of Veracity*

In *Succeed the Right Way*, Paul Gunn takes us on a journey of success through his own personal stories of human kindness, compassion, and true emotional intelligence as a leader. We get to understand what the real definition of a compassionate leader means not only in work but in life. We see in Paul's story that the true measure of success in one's life is when it works towards creating a better, happier world for us all.

Jacqueline Way | Founder 365give

Very informative! This book has taught me to embrace my empathetic nature and use it to my advantage in my business dealings. If you're interested in a heart-centric approach to growing your organization, you must read this book!

Roxanne Derhodge | Founder of the Authentic Connection Movement, Bestselling Author of *A Therapist Insider's Guide on Relationships*

Within the pages of *Succeed the Right Way*, Paul L. Gunn, Jr. explains why empathy is a crucial business advantage. Paul shares his personal experiences how having empathy has helped him succeed in business while spotlighting the importance of investing emotionally in yourself.

Aaron Vick | Author of *Leaderpreneur & Inevitable Revolutions*

What kind of a leader do you want to be? In today's environment, people are craving authenticity and connectedness more than ever—and not just in business. Paul Gunn provides a roadmap to success that activates both our hearts and our minds in achieving our business and personal goals.

Mark Nureddine | CEO, Bull Outdoor Products, Bestselling Author of *Pocket Mentor*

Succeed the Right Way offers business leaders a way forward in the wake of the COVID-19 pandemic. The old ways won't cut it anymore. Our teams and our customers are craving something deeper. Paul Gunn creates the case for a heart-centric approach to business that is both inspiring and informative.

Moritz Davidesko | Author of *Change the Story, Save the World*

Reading Paul Gunn's *Succeed the Right Way* was an eye-opening and compelling experience. Thanks to Gunn's fascinating insights I have come to view my business and my role as a leader in a new light.

Kader Sakkaria | CDO & CTO, Ruffalo Noel Levitz, Author of *Chaos by Design*

Fascinating read! For too long I've been afraid to show empathy in a business environment for fear of being perceived as weak. Paul Gunn's book really changed the way I see myself as a leader and taught me to view my vulnerability as my greatest strength.

Kevin Jackson | EO, GC GlobalNet, Bestselling Author of *Click to Transform*

Succeed the Right Way is a step-by-step guide to a more human approach to business. It is a must-read for anyone trying to make it in today's ever-changing entrepreneurial landscape.

Imran Karbhari | VP of Technology Transformation & Strategic Initiatives, Realogy, Author of *Chaos by Design*

For anyone who's experienced personal and professional setbacks, and I know that's most of us in recent years, Paul Gunn's concept of "empathetic grit" provides some much-needed perspective. This book teaches that there is great power in viewing personal tragedy as a gateway to understanding and a way to build relationships that will take your business to the next level.

Billy Hyatt | CEO & CSO, Cicayda

Succeed the Right Way is a masterclass on the value of perspective; your most devastating loss may lead to your greatest triumph, and your biggest weakness may really be your most powerful strength.

Jim Wetrich | CEO, The Wetrich Group of Companies

Great read! Paul Gunn is a seasoned entrepreneur, and his insights are as riveting as they are beneficial to business leaders at every level. I recommend this book to anyone trying to grow their organization.

Dennis Andrews | Founder, Scar Tissue, Bestselling Author of *TOO BLUE!*

Paul Gunn delivers on his promise to show business leaders how to succeed "the right way." To be the hero of your own story, you must act like one. The revelations in this book can teach you how to do just that.

Trissa Tismal-Capili | #1 International Bestselling Author, *Your True Power*

Empathy is not a weakness in business. Far from it. Reading this book provides the tools necessary to harness this super-power and use it to grow your business and enrich your life. I can't recommend it enough.

Tamara Nall | CEO & Founder, The Leading Niche

What a journey! *Succeed the Right Way* is a fascinating how-to guide for incorporating human kindness into your business for better results and a better world.

Glenn Hopper | CFO, Sandline Discovery, and Bestselling Author of *Deep Finance*

Division and isolation are hallmarks of the digital age. Paul Gunn seeks to remedy these troubling trends through empathy and human kindness. This truly was a refreshing read in today's business climate.

Shawn Johal | Business Growth Coach, Elevation Leaders, and Bestselling Author of *The Happy Leader*

Succeed the Right Way

What Every Compassionate Business Person Must Know

Paul L Gunn Jr

Published in the United States by Leaders Press.
www.leaderspress.com

ISBN 978-1-63735-094-2 (pbk)
ISBN 978-1-63735-039-3 (Amazon pbk)
ISBN 978-1-63735-095-9 (ebook)

Library of Congress Control Number: 2021910037

DEDICATION

To my Wife, Son, Daughter (Stepdaughter), my Parents, Brother, and Mother-in-law: Without your love and support it would have made this journey a much tougher plight.

This book is also dedicated to all those who are living and seek to live in a manner that inspires others to be the best version of themselves based on a foundation of empathy.

CONTENTS

CHAPTER 1

MEET PAUL L. GUNN, JR.

Empathy in business has long been seen as a weakness among the vast majority who lead and grow successful companies. It is truly an undervalued skill in its application to becoming successful in life, let alone in business. Massive success in life and business can be achieved by building a foundation based on empathy and weaving it into the fabric of your company culture. This pathway to success is often unconventional in industries not necessarily known for their application of empathy in interactions. My life experiences and the journey I've taken can possibly shed light on how it's possible to build eight figures in annual revenue and succeed the right way—with a life based on empathy.

It is my desire that those who read this book see a pathway to success for themselves or a way to pivot that will bring overall change in themselves, their teams, and their businesses. This book was also written to speak to the hearts of those youth or budding entrepreneurs who feel they may not have success in being empathetic; this is proof it can be done. I am not the first and won't be the last to take this approach.

Empathy is part of who I am at my core. There is a natural tendency for me to lean towards issues and also an inherent concern for others. Learning how to treat others was instilled in my younger brother and I from an early age by our parents. We were taught that kindness was the ultimate sign of strength. Our father was a physically imposing man with a heart larger than life; our mother was small in frame with an even bigger heart to calm and rear us with empathy. It was never shown to us as a weakness, and was often explained that it could be misunderstood by the outside world that didn't show favor to those of our demographics. Yet we were raised to know it was extremely important to become men of values and to give to others beyond what was given to us.

The recent pandemic has made many aware of the importance of what matters in the grand scheme of life. Devastating social events coupled with an acceleration of technology have created a world where connection is more critical now than ever before. Humanity has been made aware of the fragility of life and the meaning of how far acts of kindness can go in times of need. Learning from this new awareness, and implementing tools to come out of this pandemic with better people, companies, and education for our youth has become a driving purpose for me to write this book. We all have the power to interact with empathy and show kindness while attaining our goals in life. Some may need more of a push than others to recognize the value of empathy and its application in business in the new post-pandemic landscape. My journey may help serve as a guide for how you, too, may succeed the right way in being empathetic without regrets.

My desire is that my thoughts and experiences will help you thrive in this new environment, whether you are part of the old guard and must deal with the newcomers or the other way around. This book will be useful in making your business endeavors profitable and, most importantly, will make the world a better place for everyone.

I was born in Springfield, Massachusetts, and moved to Huntsville, Alabama, when I was eight years old. Externally, I likely appeared disadvantaged both socially and economically. My parents, however, spoke to my brother and I as men of value and we were taught to give back to the world despite any known prejudices we might encounter based on the labels others placed on us. We were taught to excel in the things that were held in high moral regards, including the development of a strong self-worth. That allowed us to withstand a victim mentality for the labels sometimes held against us.

My brother and I were aware of the differences and injustices of the world. We realized early on that the need to live a life based on empathy and kindness would be most in line with the biblical principles we were taught. Such a life would eventually yield the greatest success even if great monetary wealth was never achieved. My firm belief is that this very foundation was the catalyst for success in my business endeavors. The application of empathy and the ability to deal with challenges allowed me to see the need to interact with others with empathy. The understanding gained in most cases allowed me to have an advantage, if one wanted to assess this as such. Empathy is strength. It was tested and perfected during the adversity I encountered during my business and life experiences.

My parents raised my brother and me on the foundations of morality in a spiritual and wholesome household. It was important to live a life that spoke to a relationship of being well acquainted with biblical teachings for love of humanity. We were taught to seek God and Jesus first in life. These weren't mere teachings but a way of life that yielded success past what I initially set out to do in life.

My first experience owning a business was with my younger brother once he got out of the military. Our logistics and supply chain company eventually reached #67 on *Inc.'s* Fastest-growing Private Companies list. We sold the firm after it reached $50M in sales. My entrepreneurial nature and passion about helping our soldiers get home safely drove me to start another company as my brother also sought additional paths to take. My second company was another supply chain and logistics company. I named the firm KUOG Corporation. Our mission is to continue to get our military personnel home safely and to do so based on the foundations of empathy and kindness in business. Our firm proudly answers this call to support our nation and its allies. In addition, KUOG Corporation provides support during natural disasters and moves to deliver needed materials onsite as quickly as possible. Empathy is at the core of all we do, and has helped us build a foundation that has enabled us to withstand the pandemic and allow for our growth into the future.

The Strength of Empathy

There are three domains to empathy: cognitive, emotional, and compassionate. Knowing when and how to express empathy is critical in building a foundation of trust and connection. Many view empathy as a quality not necessary to succeed, but this is contrary to what some of the best revenue teams do well. My experience in both showing empathy and being viewed as weak for it has led to a great deal of success for myself. In my opinion, empathy is an important and underused tool in business. There are many reasons for this.

When you learn to really listen, you will hear much useful information. When you are able to genuinely show empathy towards others, your business will grow in the most phenomenal ways. Cognitive empathy will increase your profit margins. It is proof that your team understands the customer, employees, and vendors. Emotional empathy is a prerequisite whether on that interaction or a history of interactions.

Leading with empathy can position you to identify the weaknesses of others in business. My empathic nature has often been perceived as a weakness, yet I have frequently been able to sense when others have tried to take advantage of or completely ignore me. I was inherently aware of their actions and their tactics and blatant attacks or working behind the scenes to sabotage our loyal vendors came as no surprise to me. It is a strength to show empathy as it is still not the norm; many will show their hand based on an incorrect assumption of your weakness. In the process, you may learn of their motives before even doing business. Being empathetic is offense and defense at the same time.

Many would consider me an empath and I would agree with this assessment. It is my belief that certain characteristics were inherent in me at birth and life experiences have fine-tuned these qualities as a result of assumptions made about me. Before the recent pandemic, these qualities were most appreciated by those who came to know and work with me. I was raised to focus on others. I've learned, as I've grown older, that many others never cultivated similar attributes for fear of being identified as weak.

For example, when my wife and I went to eat breakfast at a restaurant we frequent, the first words spoken after the hostess seated us were, "Why are you not at work? Don't you have a job to go to?" It was said in the most condescending way and it was in front of my wife and her visiting family. Her family is from another country and had heard of the racism issues faced here in the US. They were in disbelief to see this in real time. Knowing others were watching, I took the opportunity to show empathy and kindness. We were polite, even though the waitress messed up a simple order. As the meal finished, I asked for the bill, wrote a kind note that she have a blessed day, and then left her a substantial tip. When my wife's family asked why I did that, I said we need to think of the position others must in to be in such a state as to verbalize such discontent.

Cognitive empathy was used to recognize someone else's issues and concerns and deliver compassionate empathy that would help heal her discontent. I believe my actions made a difference: the next time we visited the establishment, she was much kinder. It's necessary to meet people where they are. Some are having a bad day; for others, the very nature of being empathetic will been seen as a target to attack. When this happens, you have discovered another person's weakness and not the other way around. I have walked into banks and been greeted unprofessionally by bankers. Loan officers have immediately stated specific requirements before even hearing or seeing the details of my credentials. In addition, I have been told that there are banks down the street that support lower credit score candidates. Despite the emotional firestorm I feel internally, I simply breathe. In compassionate empathy, I thank them for the information. I quickly look for their name badge so I can be sure to address them properly. I calmly reach out to shake hands.

With a heartfelt response, I sometimes push back, knowing that there is a higher executive that can help me. I let them know how much I appreciate the way the bank's products support our next level of growth. I am confident in our financial position and contract backlog. It is always my plan to show compassionate empathy in my interactions. Emotionally charged responses demonstrate the lack of cognitive and compassionate empathy that others display towards me. As I show compassionate empathy, I can see that others begin to move from an emotionally charged state to one where cognitive empathy can be applied.

Compassionate empathy is a favorite tool I use to combat emotionally charged, unempathetic people. It disengages them. For those who are repelled by it they quickly move to a cognitive state to show their mental prowess. When this happens, you need to use emotional empathy to hear the tones of engagement being presented to you. You can then disengage this person with cognitive empathy based on what you have heard. Without the use of empathy, communication may result in a power struggle. In my experience, a person fighting for power immediately shows signs of insecurity. Empathy and kindness are truly a tool that gives and receives.

The argument I often hear in favor of not showing empathy is that the person doesn't want to feel weak and left looking like a fool. My response, kindly given in those cases, is that being fearful to express empathy to understand someone is also a weakness. Recent reports have shown that new sales teams will be high on hiring in education and social skills based in psychology. Keeping this old frame of thinking will expose your weakness to the "special teams" now being assembled who know how to deal with an emotionally bottled-up person who has a defensive communication style.

Every encounter with a human gives you the opportunity to make a positive impact on them. This way of thinking has brought me the deepest connections. Those in business know you need to generate revenue. Many forget, however, that there is a human on the other side of the conversation. It's important to create an authentic connection with that other person. Automated emails aren't enough to add value or create a heartfelt desire to build a relationship.

Listen First

In most business settings, the person we first meet usually isn't the real person behind the polished façade. Listening allows that real person to emerge. That's why the first piece of advice I have for anyone is learn to listen before you speak. The power from empathy comes from listening first. Actively listen to understand. Open your ears and your heart. This requires you to pause. This pause to show you are truly engaged will go a long way. If this is not a part of your "DNA," then working towards this will work wonders in your relationships. During the process you will begin to see positive responses to your actions; this will help you make the process of active listening a norm. It is my belief that once you see the responses to your actions based in empathy, it will be difficult to continue the way you behaved prior to showing it more. Listening, and truly hearing, is the first critical tool to utilize in building relationships based on empathy.

Listen and people will tell you more about themselves than you can imagine. When you are in business you must connect with people to be successful. When you actively listen, they know you care and when they know you care a bond begins to form.

Letting people speak also gives you ample opportunity to observe them. Are they looking at their watch or phone? Are they looking at someone else in the room? Maybe they're just waiting for an opening. If they abandon the conversation with barely a word, what does that tell you? Or, are they examining you too closely? Maybe they aren't making eye contact but only looking at your watch, your shoes, and even asking what kind of car you drive? Maybe they are simply sizing you up on a purely self-serving basis. People convey a lot of information with their expressions, eye movements, and body language. Listen, observe, and let them tell you what their agenda is.

If you listen long enough, you will hear what people *need* and not what their polished business façade wants. Wants and needs are two very different things. Fill someone's needs and they will never forget you.

Business is not the first thing on my mind when I approach a person. I am sincerely working to connect with that person. I strive to make lifelong connections. Whether we do business together or not, I don't care; if you are a great person, I want to get to know you. And, on a practical note, building a network of people that remember and like you is incredibly powerful. Even if they can't give you business directly, they will often know someone who can use your product or services.

When you approach an individual just wanting something in return, they can tell your intentions and will often shut down. When you really want to form a connection, and really hear what they have to say, they will be far more likely to open up and form a bond with you. That bond is everything.

It's a small world and the people you meet today might be in a very powerful position tomorrow. They will remember how you treated them in the beginning.

Empathy and the New Workplace

One good thing to come out of the COVID-19 pandemic is that people of all races and creeds are working together. We have decided that we want a different world, one where all are allowed to live their lives respected and unafraid.

Technology is allowing like-minded people all over the world to collaborate and form a new way of doing business. I believe that most people are good; technology is allowing all the good people to find each other and help each other out, at least that's what I'm seeing. As a result of this new majority of good, old ways are being challenged and refined. But, working with people from all over the world, it also means that empathy is now more important than ever.

Going online has made it so that all types of people, from every location, can have a shot at a job. They don't need to live in a certain neighborhood anymore. And we need to be aware of that as we move forward. We're all in the same boat and the only way forward is to cooperate and row together.

Being empathetic also required strategy in the perception of our firm. Cognitively I understood demographics played a role and wanted to be seen as a business rather than seeking a handout based on the color of our demographics. As an example, when we first started out, no company pictures appeared on our leadership page. As two young men of color, we wanted to succeed in our industry based on our abilities to deliver and compete. We wanted to avoid many of the roles specifically set aside for people of color. There was an early push for us to attend major conferences in person to gauge the competition. Part of our tactics were learned from a billionaire who often pretended to be unassuming support personnel to potential clients. The client's response would tell of their character and in many cases was a deal breaker it they treated the less important individuals poorly.

Another story further drives home the point: an Ivy League MBA program instructor gave his final exam after an intense semester of instruction on leadership. During the final exam, which many expected to be a long 100 question exam covering the most complex materials, he asked the students to pull out a white sheet of paper. In confusion, they proceeded. He then asked them to write the name of the janitor who cleaned in front of the two double door to the auditorium they had walked through every day for the last semester. Not one student could name him. The janitor was a kind man and the instructor made the point that if they couldn't treat individuals well who were in positions not seen to be of value then how would they be fit to lead massive corporations filled with many types of people? It would only have taken a small amount of empathy and caring to speak with the janitor and learn his name. It really brought home how often the simple things in life and business are the ones that matter most.

True leaders need this level of attention when dealing with their teams, customers, and vendors. It separates the leaders from the bosses. I believe the book *Extreme Ownership: How U.S. Navy SEALs*

Lead and Win by Jocko Willink and Leif Babin most accurately explains the benefits of empathy. Some of the toughest people on earth understand how to address austere situations with cognitive proficiency. Their empathetic approach saves lives. The mission to get the job done and everyone home safe is at the core of every Navy SEAL. They lead by taking account of the team members and by building trust. They show empathy and foster a team mentality to attack the intended goal. I recommend that you get and study this book. Navy SEALs are some of the toughest people on earth, yet they show how much you can accomplish by using empathy to create a great team.

Throw Conventional Thinking Out the Window

Conventional thinking and application in business didn't work for me. It quickly became apparent while rcsearching our business plan that we would need to find the gaps in the conventional way of doing business to be successful. We built touch points to be redirected to the offices that handled small businesses and, in the process, gained touch points to connect with later on. When we went to events, this practice enabled us to have "warm" leads or a familiar face to speak with. There was no pressure to push for outside of actually doing business with them. I wanted to test the how early deep connections made with authenticity could later develop into an invaluable connection down the road. We built real relationships in the process. When our success was obvious, we took this approach to our business interactions. We would build relationships by going after material contracts and commercial supply. These were not popular in our area at the time. When we had success with one customer we went to all the customers we could find that bought the same way and set up work that wasn't popular with other providers at that time.

Understanding that people usually follow the crowd, I wanted to know why these services weren't popular; I saw a path to build a name supporting these types of services. It later turned into massive deals. Along the way, those contacts we didn't have solutions for we kept and cultivated and were able to add value to others by making connections to other buyers who could support them. We did this without seeking anything in return because that was our way of doing business. We chose the unconventional path because it worked best for us. The theories taught in school about business and marketing didn't seem to fit the world we were living in. During the downturn of 2008-2009, we increased our marketing efforts; it had an immediate return on investment as we learned that others cut back in this area during a downturn. Our parents had often challenged us to rise above the status quo. When conventional methods didn't work, we were encouraged to make our own path. By doing that, we created our own road to success.

My father was authentic and people could tell that he was not just there for his own benefit. He was genuinely interested in others, and we learned a lot from him. Our mother taught us how diplomacy mattered in all areas, face-to-face and in writing as well. Our parents made us well aware of the important values in life. Seeing the responses from others proved just how priceless our home training and model of a father in business had been to our application of what we had learned.

A wealthy person— who was much impressed by the morals and values I had learned in my upbringing— once told me, "You can't put a price on integrity. I know I could leave you in a room overnight with a hundred million dollars and when I returned the next morning there would still be a hundred million dollars in that room." It really struck me that the focus on the values of morality and empathy was so important in business. This was education that schools didn't emphasize as being critical for success. The things that other kids made fun of me for were the very things that highly successful business executives valued the most. There were qualities you just can't pay for and it was a priceless learning experience. It showed me the value of empathy in business and I realized what my advantages really were.

Speaking of Kids

One of the blessings of the twenty-first century is the opportunity to provide your child or children with a path to life as an entrepreneur. Recent generations have been exposed to technology, remote learning, and collaborating in virtual environments. They are at the forefront of the new workplace. In the past, companies had time to go to market with a new product, but now they need to be far quicker. Those who can't keep up fall behind too quickly to recover in some cases.

The post-pandemic marketplace is shaping and realigning to require technical skills to function well. It is my belief— which is also supported by other thought leaders— that empathy, kindness, and soft skills will be critical for success in the future. Teaching our youth how to take advantage of their opportunities and work to become leaders for tomorrow starts with those in leadership roles now living the example. If our youth learn the pros and cons of entrepreneurship early, they may have the chance to show mastery in leadership and reach significant levels of success while executing within a framework of skills based in empathy. This generation, and those that follow, will understand social, political, and economic situations on a global scale. Having the tools to make a difference and the inner drive to want to do so will be what our coming generations need to succeed. As a CEO and parent, my wife and I work to pass down the qualities that will allow our children to consider a career as an entrepreneur. We leave room for them to explore their own paths, too.

My First Business

When my brother was honorably discharged from the Marine Corps following his service after 9/11, our father asked if we would ever consider going into business together. Looking back, our father is a master teacher, and this question was asked to spark interest to move us toward our true calling. Those words were enough for my brother and I to make a connection prior to his return. When the flight landed, my brother, mother, and father were there and they drove us to apartment set up in an inexpensive area. It was furnished with our mother's vanity desk and my brother's laptop. My brother later brought up in our fifth year in business that he remembered me telling him when he asked what the next steps were the day we started, and I replied with a serious smile, "We're going to develop a five-year plan and then get out of our way." The 'get out of my way' reference to him was in regard to the obstacles I knew we both would face, and we would go all in. We named the firm Gideon Services.

We utilized market research to determine what companies in our line of work were doing in revenue after one, five, and ten year marks. We adjusted our revenue goals accordingly. Our determination and focus on building a business based on empathy and kindness allowed us to reach all our milestones early. Our five-year goal was reached in three years, and our ten-year goal in seven. Part of our learning came from making mistakes. When we secured our first contract, it was with a well-known customer, and they ordered the wrong item. After review, it was determined that they had been responsible for the ordering error. Time was against us to deliver on the product for a project it supported and we didn't want to burn this bridge when we were just starting out. We paid for the correct items, with no additional charges to the customer, and had them shipped. This customer later became the critical reference in helping us secure one of our largest customers. Looking back, I am glad we resolved the issue in a way that demonstrated our business was built on acts of empathy and kindness.

The feeling of losing money on our first deal was unpleasant; it was certainly not the outcome we anticipated. In addition, seeing our customer admit fault but not take action to cover the cost was bothersome. The relationship equity gained for our actions, however, paid off more than the cost of reordering the correct material. This experience helped me learn the value in building relationships and how our actions when things didn't go as planned could be the point where our firm really excelled. From that moment on, everything we did was based on furthering our belief that empathy is how we would build our reputation; we would not change who we were to succeed. It made it easier for us to know that when things didn't go as planned, there would be no second guessing or changing our character as to how we would handle situations. This way of operating allowed us to reach #67 on *Inc.'s* Fastest-growing Private Companies list in 2014. This way of doing business reflected who I am and business became an extension of the value held in my personal life.

After marriage and the birth of our son, I wanted to ensure that my time was focused on being the best husband and father I could be. My brother and I had built a very successful company, but we decided to sell it so we could focus on the things we deemed important for the next phase of our lives. For me, this was family. The time spent with them made me realize that my purpose was to leave a legacy for our family and children to become moral leaders. Their learning would best come from observing my behavior in the same way my brother and I saw our parents actions while growing up. The dual purposes for supporting our military personnel and this drive to leave a legacy drove me to start KUOG Corporation. I had learned many lessons from my previous company; this time I wanted to do something more hands-off, so I started a business to help other people become a source of supply for the federal government. In working with these firms, I came to realize that many simply didn't want to deal with the paperwork involved in becoming a government supplier.

Our previous firm was built on such a strong foundation that our loyal contacts went beyond business. Our success was based on helping others ultimately support a larger purpose: to help our military personnel have what they need so they could get home safely. The confidence from our previous success and knowing firsthand how empathy and kindness could build a strong brand allowed me to push through the trials of growing a new firm and find success. The new company also served disaster areas. This involved faster response items, as you can imagine. When something like a hurricane or other natural disaster hits, you don't have time to squabble over pennies. You have to get people what they need as quickly as possible.

What I Do Now

My field of expertise is supply chain management. I lead teams in the execution of deliverables to ensure materials are delivered to our military end users. My career was developed around procurement, logistics, and supply chain. I have been able to reach a great deal of success in this domain. My current company appeared on *Inc.'s* Fastest-growing Private Companies list in 2021 at number #273. Some of the skills I utilize on a daily basis to succeed include consulting, training, and project management implementing quality management, continuous improvement, and technology solutions for global organizations leading cross-functional teams in Asia, Europe, the Middle East, and America. I play a major part in ensuring our military personnel have the materials they need to get home safely. Many would consider me an SME (Subject Matter Expert), driving all project phases from proposal generation and requirements gathering to planning and execution.

I led one of my former firm's largest quality management systems (QMS) implementation and certification projects for multi-million dollar sustainment maintenance programs for highly visible DoD (Department of Defense) end users. I hold a Bachelor of Arts in Sociology from Georgia State University and a Master of Science in Business Administration from the University of Phoenix. I am also the founder of Watertusk Corporation, a company that supplies materials for those who want a premium outdoor experience.

As the founder of KUOG Corporation (KUOG), empathy is integrated into all we do. Woven in the fabric of our existence are empathetic actions that sustain, deliver, and acquire materials to support our mission. We are a supplier of choice to the federal government and private sector when crisis strikes, sustainment is needed, or on-time delivery is a must. Strategically designed to deliver fast, reliable, and quality materials, our reliability is the cornerstone of our operations because ultimately someone is depending on the success of our system working. The company offers customers greater flexibility and improved control over the flow and inventory of products and materials. I am proud of being able to deliver components, equipment, and materials wherever, whenever, and however my customers need them.

As a prime contractor to the federal government, we have provided support to large complex agencies such as the Navy Corona Division Naval Surface Warfare Center Dahlgren Division, Navy Special Operations Command (SOCOM), National Aeronautics and Space Administration (NASA), United States Army Letterkenny, and the United States Marine Corps (USMC).

Why I Do What I Do

Others have deemed me a servant leader. I don't think I could be any other way. Supporting our military personnel and getting them what they need to return home safely is what drives me every day. Having seen my brother and others serve, my desire was always for their safe return. Military personnel don't just serve their families, they serve us all. This became even clearer for me when we were setting up the internet in our home. The company representative and I were speaking; they let me know they had served and were in one of the items we provided that saved their life. Their extreme thanks went on for five minutes. I internalized this event. It awoke every fiber of my being and made me want to become to be a premier supplier to the DoD and help save lives. I've never looked back.

A Logistician for Humanity

The work I do is important because it saves lives. The importance of having excellent supplier support for our military ensures they are positioned well to complete their missions. In addition, the company also serves disaster areas. It's about more than just materials. In short, I view this job as being a logistician for humanity: our work is to deliver supplies to save lives.

Working With My Brother

Contrary to what business experts say—that working with family can be disastrous and not worth the risk—my brother and I had success in our previous venture and were blessed to have the opportunity to do it together. Our experience solidified my belief that when the bond between siblings has been tested and proven, that bond can be far stronger than traditional partnerships.

How someone reacts to adversity reveals a great deal about them. When two people go through the same adverse circumstances, they can come out with similar strengths and outlooks. As a result, a strong bond is formed. You know you can count on them based on a very intimate knowledge of their dependability and reactions when things get tough.

My younger brother and I are extremely close. He was there for me from the beginning, and we've been through countless ups and downs together. We have had each other's backs for as long as I can remember. When we work together, his strengths support mine. He can see things from a different angle than I can. He can temper my moods. Our partnership is key to our growth and operations.

Business is filled with tough situations that will cloud your vision, and it helps to have someone by your side who understands you and can help you through. A close sibling will know you on a level that can help you weather current and future trials that might otherwise cause you to reach a breaking point. Your sibling can reel you in and refocus you on your goals. They aren't just going to look out for you because there is a monetary benefit; they look out for your best interest as their loved one. You may have other loyal employees and partners, but you can't pay for this type of relationship. Money can come and go, but having someone in your corner when you take your worst hit or setback is priceless.

In my case, I have a brother with whom I am blessed to have a close relationship.

Our success as business partners can be attributed to our complementary strengths and weaknesses. When making decisions, his feedback was vital; I knew I could trust his decisions. Working in the office together and getting things done, or bouncing ideas off him for plans for the future was an important aspect of our success. Your siblings' character and ability to handle tough breaks are vital aspects of their ability to ensure they are helping you grow the firm. Don't underestimate the hidden strengths they've developed from being in the trenches with you. They will have the most realistic and historical view on how you can handle any situation; they can be there to help you through tough times should you need their assistance.

On the surface, this may appear to be simple advice. However, it goes much deeper: you need to know your sibling(s), their capabilities, fit, and how they will support you for the long haul. You have to know what you want and know you need this person in your corner.

Purpose Drives My Success

Purpose is what drives me to want to succeed at what we do every day. Empathy as the foundation for our operations steers us to deliver what is needed to support our mission. The success of our firm brings me joy because it is a reminder that you can build a company, live by your morals, and succeed with empathy to impact others. There are those in business whose primary focus is to profit by all means necessary using a method that dehumanizes others in the process. They seek to be a boss instead of a leader. Knowing that we are helping to save lives and helping warfighters return home safely while doing this work brings me an immense amount of joy.

While my brother was overseas, the importance of providing the best equipment and tools to ensure he returned home safely was often on my mind. I'm sure this same concern is often on the minds of those who have family who are serving or who have served in the military. When the opportunity presented itself to be part of the supply chain to support our military, I jumped at the chance. Knowing that someone's family member is on the other side of an order or contract was bigger than simply making money. The excellence in delivery mattered. My calling was found and it is something I wake up daily ready to support against all odds. There was a personal drive for me to become a supplier that brought value and, in the process, assisted in saving money to the end user without sacrificing delivery timelines. This also ensured soldiers didn't have to go into their missions without the equipment they needed to complete their assignments.

The human connection to others in life and business is what makes this fun for me. Engagement with others matters and the authenticity in how you speak to others is crucial. How many times has someone asked you how you are doing? Now, how many times did they mean it? Did they listen to your answer? Most people say a lot of things they don't really mean. They ask questions they don't expect or want an answer to. After I saw the way people had a limited desire to genuinely connect with others, it was my stubborn position that I would continue working within my personal values and empathetic mindset. This meant that any engagement was coming from a genuine place. When I asked, "How you are doing?" I meant it. Hearing the customer's or vendor's response was the goal for me and it was a relentless pursuit to achieve this in every interaction. Building a relationship beyond business was key for me in getting to really know my customers and vendors.

This is not a one size fits all approach. Speaking frankly, sometimes people want a no-nonsense 'let's get this done' interaction. Mastery in empathy will allow for cognitive recognition of which type of person you are engaging with to understand if this is the case. Cognitive understanding of this will only make you a better leader and help you to identify the things that matter when supporting this type of customer.

Meet people where they are. That's what I do.

For example, a vendor I needed to deal with was old-school, clean-cut, and well dressed. He was an aeronautical engineer and very precise. When engaging with his front office team the first time, one of them told me, "Paul, he's old-school." That's all they said to me, and I knew to forego the standard polo shirt/slacks combination and to wear a shirt and tie. This man wasn't arrogant; he was just from an era where you dressed up to meet someone, especially your elder. After that meeting, he thanked me for wearing a shirt and tie. He said he gets people in his office who think they don't need to dress up, and it always lowers his opinion of them just a bit.

Sometimes you have to do a little digging, but you can always find something to talk about, some way to behave—something to bond over or be appreciated for.

My Hopes for Future Generations

It is my deepest desire that we can get to a point where we all want to take care of each other. People don't seem to understand that you don't have to be a pushover to be kind and compassionate. Too many people think they have to be tough and strike first. It doesn't have to be that way. I'm living proof. You can do business with a greater level of kindness and still succeed. If we could put aside our differences for one day, we could change the world. If we really helped each other, we would no longer have the need to argue over political parties or the issues that divide us. They would cease to be concerns.

My Desire for You, the Reader

It is my desire that you work to apply at least some of what you learn in this book in your personal and business life. It is my desire the lessons learned help you find success and I hope that you share that success, too. Many people are more successful than I am; they shared their success with me, and I am extremely grateful. Remember, sometimes the most valuable thing you can get from a wealthy person isn't their money; it's their time. If you have the opportunity, take advantage of their time and ask how they got to where they are now. Listen, and you will likely get a priceless education.

CHAPTER 2

A MINDSET OF CARING

Philosophy of Empathy

Empathy is a way of life for how I live and seek to inspire others in business. This way of living in the business setting with empathy as a foundational building block for our firm has yielded the greatest results for us. In the process I made deep and lasting connections that go beyond business. In my opinion and experience, showing empathy in business is still widely perceived as weakness. Being vulnerable in business may be considered a cardinal sin by those who are closed to viewing business built on empathetic actions. I have been able to build two successful firms based on this way of living and I think it could be very valuable to others, too.

When it comes to business deals and monetary transactions, being seen as weak may make one feel vulnerable. No one wants to feel this way. A worldwide phenomenon took place during the COVID-19 pandemic that accelerated the awareness to the need to adjust and change the old ways of thinking and begin to show more empathy in business. There appears to have been an awakening to challenge the status quo and begin to call out actions of those in positions of leadership. The old ways of thinking placed an emphasis on working towards the bottom line. The needs of individuals are placed at the bottom of the list, if considered at all. It is my opinion, as we move out of the pandemic, that people will demand that leaders take accountability and lead from positions of empathy.

History may hold a different view on this. In the past, the mindset of showing no weakness and only the strong survived was the way to succeed. It is my view this concept and way of life was incorrect. Those who are wise collaborate and build teams to outperform their competitors via strong alliances. This is done well when relationships are formed and nurtured with empathy. Previously, many operated from positions of brute strength; there was not time or ability for a discussion to accurately size up the situation. The use of fear was perceived to be a strength. Even now it is sometimes utilized in business settings. The current world, for the most part, doesn't operate that way anymore. My personal belief is that business has always been a mental game. Mastery of emotions and how to reframe situations are found in many who understand the importance of empathy. Its application in business can yield significant results. Taking a serious dive into understanding why empathy in business works would be a wise move to better position yourself and your company for any future endeavors.

Conscious and unconscious bias still exist; overlooking this fact would be naïve. Those high in emotional intelligence recognize that fear associated with a bias is typically rooted in the internal issues and experiences of those who hold them. Fear is the basis for so many of our issues. Most people know it's wrong to judge others on things they can't change such as race or gender. As technology helps bring the world closer together, we are hopefully going to see those differences more clearly and dispel much of our fear. Being empathetic and leading to inspire others will be an important skill. Asking someone how their day is going and taking time to really listen won't reduce your perceived strength. It may actually do the reverse. Those types of encounters can help you change perceptions and dispel fear. Choosing to live a life rooted in empathy and a mastery of soft skills like interpersonal communication will help you create authentic and life-changing experiences with others.

It's extremely difficult to fake empathy. People don't like to be lied to. Authenticity matters when connecting with others. People know they can't trust a liar, and faking things like empathy really upsets people when they realize your intentions are false. It creates a backlash that can be far worse because they think you are insulting their intelligence.

Humans have the capability to be empathetic. Hardship and loss ignite some people to reach this position sooner than others. Many are deeply rooted in a belief to not show vulnerability. Once they have experienced the positive effects on them, however, they may move to take this way of living as a possible path forward. Vulnerability leads to a path of deep connection. Showing empathy in business may actually position you to be more successful. The uncomfortable situations that I have been in assisted me in refining my soft skills. They helped me learn how to be empathetic in business dealings and determine whether people were genuinely good people who may need to learn they can trust me, or people I should keep an eye on.

In the pre-pandemic world, the standard response when asking people how they were was either fine or okay; people were frequently on autopilot. Once they realized the genuineness in my asking, it often took them some effort to adjust their tone or demeanor. In most cases, individuals came to appreciate my asking the genuine question. Post pandemic, there is an emotional charge when this question is asked, and people are more likely to respond honestly. When you ask how a person is doing, be prepared to hear someone's response. This is critical when you first engage because if this is not a natural character trait, you have to work on ensuring you are doing your best to mean it. You're better off not asking a question than asking and not listening to the reply. If you ask a question and tune out the answer, or worse, talk over the person, you're making a point of telling them that you don't care. You will come across as not being authentic and may appear emotional challenged for showing a lack of empathy and kindness.

Priorities have changed. People are far more comfortable sharing their personal lives and talking about the challenges they are facing. I've seen more friendships develop because of the remote work we are doing. In the past, it would have been unthinkable to conduct business on a video call with kids and animals in the background. But people are isolated, and when they have the chance to interact with someone, they make it count. Show empathy and it will make for adventurous times.

When big business shifts, everyone else falls in line. When leaders in large corporations show kindness and empathy as a way of life, their actions will cause a ripple effect. Corporations are finally beginning to realize what they're doing to the world, what they're doing to the economy. Leaders in small businesses can help solidify the trend toward a more positive and engaging world.

Generation Alpha

The generation born between 2010 and 2024 is called Generation Alpha. Their number one trait is learning and growing up in a society where technology has been a part of their entire lives. As a business community and society, we have a wonderful opportunity to move towards a way of life based on a philosophy of empathy. Tech is changing how we interact. As a result of the pandemic and advances in technology, we have seen the birth of the cancel culture. People are becoming more mindful of how they interact with one another. This is in part based on the fear of knowing there might be social ramifications for any actions, instead of primarily being concerned for others for a genuine reason. It is great that society is becoming more aware. This is truly an opportunity to show why operating on a foundation of empathy will lead one far in business. You can't get away with bad behavior anymore. You're always on the record. This shouldn't be the reason for seeking to "appear" empathetic, however. Be authentic and simply show interest in connecting with others. You may miss the mark at first but you'll learn how to perfect your communication as you do it more frequently. The deep connections you make and the growth your firm will attain seeking to succeed the right way will be worth your efforts in the end.

You probably studied how your parents interacted with people. With that said, a ten-year-old often doesn't have the depth of thought to apply what they learned from their parents directly to business situations. This knowledge develops as you have experiences, especially experiences going into business basically run by, it seems, wealthy men. Being two young men of color, my brother and I have had experiences that helped develop our philosophy regarding kindness and empathy toward others. But so much was developed because it is the way I was raised... and it's just the way that I am.

Born Empathetic

It is my belief, based on identified characteristics, that I am an empath. I strongly identify with some of the tendencies. Being empathetic comes naturally to me. The additional cues and insights that I pick up in conversations usually don't stray too far from the first impressions assessed when I make initial contact with people. These qualities were further fostered in a home life high on morality; I didn't just learn about empathy and caring but was encouraged to live out the values to the best of my ability. The home environment is extremely critical in setting the path toward building humans that will be leaders in this world. What happens in the home and early years matters for the imprinting of personality. Aristotle was quoted as saying, "Give me a child until he is 7 and I will show you the man." Research in neuroscience backs this up. Children from a stable home, with parents that focus on the importance of treating others with kindness and empathy, develop into adults who are more likely to do the same. It's not my intention to fault children from rough demographics who might not have the advantages of the same upbringing. The experiences they endure may also be a catalyst to help those who've lived that life to use empathy as a skill to know who is safe for them.

At a certain age, your mind is developed and set. Anything after that requires retraining of the brain. You repeatedly act on things the way you have set in stone by the time you're a young person. But you can change; people do it all the time. It takes effort, but you can change your nature. When that happens, you'll see life differently based on the way people interact.

Listen, Learn, Discern

Listening is a critical pillar in empathy. In my interactions, it's obvious that people want to be listened to, heard, and understood. For this to provide optimum effectiveness one must be able to actively listen to others. Connecting with others can start off on a good footing if you ask open-ended questions such as, "How does that make you feel?" or "What resonates or bothered you about that situation?" etc. Allow the person to speak and share. Be attentive in the listening. When people talk about themselves without asking about others, it may make the connection more difficult create on the front end. Actively listening will allow for them to talk more and the more you listen, the more you hear about them, and they will eventually begin to sense the genuineness in your communication with them. When someone else shares their thoughts or feedback, it is an opportunity for them to open up and bond with you. This world thrives off of human connection. In business, it's no different. There are many cues given in conversation that are passed on if you listen carefully. These cues can help you sense what others may need; cognitive empathy can help you understand how best to support them. It takes emotional empathy for you to assess the strengths, weaknesses, threat level, wants, and desires of others, then deliver with compassionate empathy the eventual solutions based on the intel from cognitive empathy.

My life has proven the hypothesis that conducting business with empathy is a way to build a business and succeed the right way. Many times, I asked myself, does this work living like this and acting like that? Those thoughts would race through my head and say, "Well, life is going to test this, so let's prove it to be true." It was my belief that success could be achieved and I was determined to make it a reality. It is often said that everyone has a price. Knowing this, I took this as a jab at character, knowing that those whose lives are based in morality may see this as referencing those who do not live with morality. People bend and move based on what's put in front of them.

Impacting and inspiring others by way of living with empathy and kindness will keep your mind focused on actions that are typically difficult to put a price on. Walking a life based in morals usually keeps you grounded. The purpose driving you to succeed goes beyond the money.

For example, there was a highly visible project we were working on. Our customer had a preferred source. The supplier utilized a supplier of our choice that we had built a relationship with based on empathy. The preferred source was upset when they were made aware that we had won the deal. We initially weren't in their circle of partners. They called our firm and were rude to our operations manager. The individual asked to speak to me then immediately started yelling profanity at me, saying it was his contract and that he could do me a favor. His favor was to come visit me, take the work, and then give me what he thought was 5 percent of the deal and he would pay me when he felt like it.

It was a threatening call. Most people told me I should have hung up. I wanted to see where this would go and understand their position for losing. It's not a fun position to be in when you lose a major deal. After he finished yelling, I let him know he could most certainly could come visit us. It would be lovely. He really got upset and continued to yell due to how calm I was with my response. Shortly after I let him know I understood his frustration, I asked what their primary line of work was. I inquired if there was a possibility to work with us in conjunction with our other source. He immediately calmed down.

He proceeded to go on about all his firm's offerings. Then, the more he talked, the more he went on about how his position was win or no collaboration. That was when I knew this person was not going to accept working with us, no matter what was done aside from his firm securing the deal. I let him know if his position changed, we would be happy to revisit this. The sense from the call was that this person was out to cause a real issue. Ultimately, he tried to get to another distributor to delay shipments for specific parts. But our partnerships were strong. They were built on trust, empathy, and kindness.

When I noticed what had been done, I went to the company and said, "This situation is certainly something. I understand you're not pleased. This effort is for the greater good of others. At this point, it's not about the money. Are you able to put aside the bad feelings and help those on the other end of this?" They didn't care. They said, "No, we're not doing it." This was a very large company; they were upset they didn't get what they wanted and they refused to help us.

The weight of our customer and the resources at their disposal to help step in when this type of situation happens was always at our beck and call. There was urgency on this effort, so there was a limited time available to get the job done. Now, I knew that our customer had rules where I could tell them they have a certain number of days to do something and, if they don't want to do it, we'll come and step in. I told them, "All right, you all have six days, will you help and consider it?"

I never told them I had the full weight of the customer's resources behind me. I just went in and said, "Just consider the situation." I took an empathetic approach, but I had to get the customer involved to make them execute it. It took a combination of cognitive and compassionate empathy to get this task done. Cognitive empathy was applied by understanding they would not bend to the situation without the weight of the customer's assistance. Compassionate empathy was applied by understanding that there was frustration on their end which warranted us to think in their shoes and deliver a response that showed we cared. On top of that, I got them another deal that cost me money. I had to pay more so they could get a specific order, but they still showed that they were an unethical company. The evidence for their behavior was shown at the front end; the way they acted in the beginning showed how they would behave in the long run. If they weren't willing to bend because it was the right thing to do, chances are they weren't ever going to change their mindset. Our actions and our attempts to show care and consideration, however, were still an opportunity to leave a positive memory for them. They may never forget our example, despite how they acted in the moment.

I could see if the actions had come from a mom-and-pop shop, like, "Well, I just can't do it because we need this." That's somewhat understandable, due to the nature of limited resources and efforts to secure news clients. But doing it, or choosing not to, just shows the character of the people you're dealing with, and that doesn't change overnight.

It's amazing that a business can act that way. The mindset that if they can't have the business then no one else will is extremely petty. I'm glad I didn't threaten them. I talked to them with sincere empathy, and asked them to do the right thing.

Sometimes people live life another way. They think that they can go up and down, choose when they want to be empathetic. You can't choose when to do right or wrong. You have to have that as a kind of a constant stability, and then you can learn from trial and error who does what. It's not in line with the path you want to travel, but if you want to do and have some staying power, you're going do it.

Where are the Bullies Now?

Much of our mindset has changed because of the pandemic. If you even think about it, where are the bullies in school now, the mean people who randomly met and formed an alliance to ostracize others? They can't mess with the kid down the hallway if they're not there anymore.

I've had a lot of success, but there are times that this philosophy of empathy loses out. In this post-pandemic world, however, I see less of that. People are more willing to work with someone like me. Business isn't just about maximum profit anymore. Things are shifting. But there will be those that don't change, like an individual I worked with recently.

I needed an item only made by one source. When I asked the person to accommodate my shipping needs, he was like, "No, tell the customer to come get it." I was taken back, but told him, "They're not buying it that way. They won't buy it." His response blew me away. He straight up said, "I don't care!"

I asked him if he could at least honor the price he quoted me, and he said, "Well, I'm God. I'm God to your customer, and I'm God to you, so I will charge anything that I *bleep, bleep, bleep* feel like." Wow! I thought...just wow. I said, "All right, man. I understand that. But can you honor this, please?" His response was, "Well, I will honor the price, but that's it. That's all I'm going to do. I'm God."

I'll never forget that. I've heard some crazy stuff, but "I am God" is above and beyond everything else. It's clear that there are people that just don't care.

Value First, Money Later

This reminds me that it's important for the focus to be on value first, and money later. One thing I've learned in most cases is that money comes after the value. Those who have been successful focus on bringing value first. They learn to know and understand people. They know that you can't build value without others believing you can. People need to trust you. Success follows when people trust you to do what you say. Sometimes you have to work with challenging personalities, and play really tough, but you don't reach certain levels of wealth without having others respect you and know that you are trustworthy. These people respond well to genuine empathy and may be gained as true allies with proper application of empathy.

To get any kind of a business deal, you essentially have to prove yourself before actually working to make the deal happen. That's why my theory is to give information out for free, or a portion of what you can for free. Let people see the value you offer. Share the value and help people and they will think, "If you're giving this away for free, what else do you know that can really help me?"

If you see a kid starting out in business who has no money and is asking for advice, maybe you give this kid advice for free. If a billion dollar company asks for your advice, you're going to charge them your normal fee. You're not overcharging them, you're providing value to help that company, the same way you don't charge a young person that you're working to help who has nothing. You look at the situation and assess: what's the right thing to do? The correct answer is determined case by case.

If you are in a cash-poor situation, it's difficult to focus on the long-term and creating value. If you actually need the sale, it can be tough. I was in this position. When we started out, we needed every penny. But if you're going to stay for the long term, you have to act carefully in the short term. That's when you most need to do things right. Your short-term actions will often determine your long-term success at the same time.

And you're not putting on airs, you're telling people who you are and the value that you bring. That's going to be the same value position even when you become successful. Dollar values many change over time but the process for being empathetic will not. You should be the same way you are the first time you meet someone as when you've established a lasting relationship with them. They'll get to know you and believe in you and, even when something goes wrong, they'll know and trust you to handle it.

Transparency is important in every situation. Money versus value. Part of that value is being clear and honest. One of our clients came to look at our internal process. They asked us what we do when we bid. I told them and his reply was, "You know, nobody does that in your industry—or at least very few." I felt like, why would I do anything differently? If you want to do business with me and you want to know something about my company, I'm going to tell you.

He could see that I was breeding trust, but he didn't know that I never thought of it that way. That's just the way I am. If you don't like what you see, then there's nothing I can do. I'm not going to lie or work and trick you. If you want me to change a foundational piece about me, then you're going to have to walk away.

The way I see it, if you have to walk from something because it conflicts with your values, you walk away. Own your values, don't compromise. Some people can operate with the mindset of, "I want it so bad; I'll do anything to get it." Well, that's their value base. It may work for them, but not for me. There are many things more important to me than money. There are lines I won't cross. If you are not clear on those lines for yourself, you can find yourself in a situation where you have to choose. If you are unprepared, you can make a really bad mistake.

We used to tell our customers our actual costs and show them everything in between. They didn't expect that much detail, but we gave it to them anyway. We would tell the customer who the vendor was, and they could go and do their own due diligence if they wanted. I've gotten better at assessing people on a case-by-case basis so I can determine whether they are legitimately inquiring about business or fishing for information. But having built transparency and trust with customers, things move much faster. If a new person at a company we're dealing with comes to me with questions, I feel comfortable telling them to go and ask their boss. There's no need to prove myself over and over.

But these relationships are forged over time; they require a great deal of effort. I essentially gave people a roadmap to the work I do and if they wanted to, they could have cut me out of the process. But I know my value. The deals I make, putting the entire process together, is my strongest skill. It's like a musician handing you an instrument and the sheet music. Technically, you can play the song, but people in business know that you get what you pay for. They don't have time to learn a new instrument. It's more cost effective for them to pay me to do what I do and when I'm transparent they know what they are getting, and they know they can trust me. That's a priceless asset for people with real money. Anybody can sell a house, but there's a reason we get agents to do it and pay them for their service.

And that leads me to the fact that everyone has the same number of hours in a day. People who get a lot done know how to delegate.

Everyone Has the Same Twenty-four Hours

I met a billionaire and realized that this guy has the same twenty-four hours in a day that I do. But what really hit me was the way he acted with people. He still had passion, he still had grit, he still was a no-nonsense guy, but he was never someone that looked down on you. He treated everyone with respect. I remember thinking that if this guy can make a billion starting from nothing, then I can make it to a much higher level. That was my eye-opener.

I realized that everything I had been taught about success in business was wrong. I was taught that you couldn't have money or get a certain job if you didn't go to a certain school. You couldn't be forthright and honest in business. This man right in front of me was living proof that none of that was true. I don't need to lie on a job application to get a job. I can tell the truth. I didn't really know that until I got around that guy. I was blown away to realize that not only does being yourself work, but successful people appreciate your authenticity. This guy was himself and became a billionaire doing things his way; he had multiple businesses and hired many people to help him succeed. I realized I didn't need to know everything,

I just needed to hire the right people and put them where they needed to be.

When you are unable to listen to people and hear what they are saying, it will make it more difficult to get to know them. Learning something new from them will certainly be that much more difficult. Someone who has a deep understanding of empathy and who is willing to be transparent with others will make significant impacts on those they encounter. It most often requires a high level of emotional intelligence to interact with other people this way.

When I met this man, everything clicked, and I decided that that was how I was going to handle my business.

How My Father Handled Wealthy People

Growing up and watching my father interact with other affluent business professionals allowed me to see firsthand how leading with morals was a strong way to build relationships in business. It certainly opened my eyes and gave me a leg up. Listening to others is what I most often saw as the key trait my father excelled at beyond his proficient skill with numbers. He was able to make people very comfortable because of how they were able to speak and be heard. His advice came from the heart, and he showed genuine care for others. His character was easily visible in his encounters. I would argue most people knew who they were dealing with in their first interaction. These are the same qualities I want to pass on to our son as he sees me interact with others. My father wasn't seeking anything in return beyond the value of what he was giving in help. He built real relationships with people and money was not the basis.

My dad was a straight shooter, a New Yorker at heart. His goodwill and humor were evident in his smile. He didn't sugarcoat things, but he wasn't rude either. He was who he was, and people could count on him. People frequently bonded with him instantly and it was very rare that he didn't make an initial bond immediately.

The moment people first engage with you, they are assessing your authenticity and intended motives. Whether conscious or subconscious, this assessment happens very quickly. Significant data exists regarding how quickly the brain assesses if someone is a friend or foe. You may only have five seconds to capture this information. Running a business with your morals in place allows for others to sense and see the authenticity in your tone, communications, and actions. Acting with kindness and empathy will make it difficult for anyone to perceive you as a threat in these five seconds. Your nonverbal cues will tell them you are a friend and not a foe. Kindness and empathy will deepen your connections. It did for me, and I am certain it will for you as well.

Kind Versus Nice

Experience has taught me that people confuse kind and nice or consider them the same word. The dictionary describes them as two different things. Being nice means that you are polite and act pleasant (act being the important word). Being kind means that you actually care about people, and you show that you care. You can be very nice to someone while doing them wrong, or you can be kind to someone and not be very nice about it. It sounds odd, but you can be nice to someone and still be unkind.

Many people confuse me for being nice until they are put in a position with me to be shown empathy without my being nice. This looks like showing a strong response with cognitive empathy for understanding the situation and delivering compassionate empathy. Compassion is shown with immovable delivery due to it usually being based on a moral premise. To the untrained eye of someone who is lacking emotional intelligence, it is taken as not being nice or as rash in judgment. Being kind is a strength often overlooked. Showing kindness will address a tough situation with good use of cognitive empathy and deliver the solution with compassion despite how emotional the other(s) might be.

Nice will agree with others to be liked and in the process override compassion and cognitive empathy because that person is only focusing on emotional triggers for themselves while completely ignoring the cognitive application and ability to support others with compassion. Nice usually doesn't cut it unless you are giving out treats at the workplace. Kind wins most of the time. For example, when being kind to someone you will hear their point of view, disagree, and then act so the that the end user receives the accurate solution. You're typically not concerned whether you were nice but only did you meet the solution and in the process show kindness as a leader to impact the team for the future.

Agreeableness, or being nice, can hinder goals and business due to a tendency to not act with a high level of cognitive empathy. Niceness usually lacks compassionate empathy because it is only concerned about doing the right thing for fear of emotional backlash.

In my opinion, parenthood is much like kind versus nice. You have to be kind with your kids, but that doesn't mean you have to be nice and let them do everything they want to do. You can be very kind to them while still thinking of the overall goals you have for them. It's good to be nice, but you have to stop kids from hurting themselves and others.

The book *Extreme Ownership* emphasizes the need to be the leader, to take full responsibility. People might say you are not nice, because they didn't get what they want, but you are being kind even if is not seen in that moment. If you feel the need to explain, let them know you understand how they feel that you were not being nice. Acknowledge their feelings, then state briefly that your actions were based on kindness for all.

Teams that work on the premise of actions primarily dominated by being nice tend to fail on projects. They are usually lacking a team member high in emotional intelligence who can speak and lead with kindness to enact change to get the job done. Someone high in cognitive empathy would have recognized the flaw and acted on this with compassionate empathy. If making people feel good in the short term is your goal and you lack emotional strength, then being nice may be your suitor. It is much wiser to act with kindness even if it feels as though you won't be liked if you know that cognitively it is best for all. You are doing the right thing for everyone. Being agreeable isn't what a leader needs to be. Being kind allows a leader to show kindness and empathy while still making the hard choices and decisions.

Warren Buffett says, "The difference between successful people and really successful people is that really successful people say no to almost everything." Get to the point where you can say no to anyone. Looking at it closer, you can see how kindness can propel a person in business, while nice can hold them back. It's a case where being kind can mean telling someone no for a larger purpose. Be kind, but not so nice that you take too much stuff on. There were times early in my career where I was guilty of confusing nice with kind to the detriment of a project. I wanted to be nice and realized later that it wasn't the correct thing to do for me or everyone else. I had to learn that being kind was better than being nice. It's a philosophy I work to live by.

This is an important distinction. If you insist on being nice over being kind, there will be consequences. If you are being nice just to avoid confrontation, you are really not avoiding the confrontation just actually delaying it. Like a dam holding back water, it will grow larger and larger. There is no avoiding confrontation in my mind. You are only putting it off and letting it grow.

In the firm I co-owned with my younger brother, we split duties based on the skills we were best at. Empathy and kindness in sales were my strong points; his was the ability to assess threats to the firm from those who viewed empathy and kindness as a weakness. As a Marine, he was keen on leadership and we worked well together. I went after sales contracts with a focus on kindness and empathy. He made sure the contracts were followed and that things got done correctly. I knew he had my back. We enjoyed working this way and our customers appreciated the way business was handled. My brother knew how to be very direct, and he was never worried about being nice. It was a winning combination. Some people need help balancing being kind and direct, and some people can do it all on their own. My advice would be to just make sure that balance happens by moving between emotional, cognitive, and compassionate empathy. This is a long-term strategy that is rooted in growth and sustainment. Its prerequisite is going to require that you slow down and back away from the mindset of hurrying to get sales and grow.

How do you do that? How do you decide when you are taking on too much because you are being too nice? Obviously, you don't want your agreeableness to end up as a negative. You want to help people, but you don't want to be taken advantage of and you don't want to destroy your business. Making good decisions can be difficult at first, especially when the financial benefits are saying so at a high level without considering all the costs. There will be times you make a misstep. It can be difficult to learn to let go of thinking and feeling a certain way. That's why it's important to slow down and think because your natural tendencies can override your decisions in the moment. It's a fine line between being kind and nice; it is wise to cognitively assess the situations and know when to temper the two.

For those of you just starting out, you might think you have to do everything yourself. Be kind, and as you grow, as you hire people, make sure that you hire people with complementary skills. Make sure your team can temper and balance you. Your teams are less likely to benefit when you build entire units with nice people who will avoid confrontation. It is wiser to identify kind people. These are the people who are going to utilize all domains of empathy to deliver solutions even if it means speaking harsh truths.

Look for those people who will challenge your viewpoints and question what you're doing, especially in the early stages. The early stages are when you are going to identify a person's abilities. You need to know what a person's kind-to-nice balance is and also if they are going to stay on mission. From my experience, I know I am looking for team members who can show empathy and understand the foundation of it without confusing it with being nice but rather kind. These are those who may appear nice, but still waters run deep; should they need to, they will delegate work and will lead with excellence and empathy.

As an example, a CEO might have two advisors: one of them is a yes person. They always back up the leader. Their relationship with this leader is very pleasant and easygoing. This team member says yes to almost everything, without reason or feedback, just to be nice. The other person has some conflict with this leader but is kind and gives accurate and often prescient information in a compassionate way despite how they feel emotionally about the leader. Why is it that that person being kind will lead to more positive results than the person who's always supporting the leader and just being nice? Because they're going to tell the leader when he sidesteps. They're going to have the empathy to know you're stepping out of line as a CEO and tell you. It may not appear to be nice telling you this, but they're being kind. They're not thinking about themselves, they're thinking about the people in the family of your business. It is critical in business to know who you can trust, both in interactions with customers and team members. You need to know who is able to act with empathy over being nice. It matters because stuff's going to hit the fan in business; you're going to make wrong decisions or pick a bad vendor, or a vendor does something wrong and doesn't deliver.

In a leadership role, taking ownership is showing empathy and kindness. You are going to have to be the one to own up to the good and the bad. When something goes wrong, you're going to have to be the one to go to the customer. You will have to say that you were in control, you were at the helm, and any mistakes made were your responsibility. If you only have nice people around, you are most likely not placing your team in the best position to succeed. That person who notes conflict, they're being kind.

When they tell you about issues, they're actually providing you with important information and allowing you to make the best decisions.

If you have a yes person just telling you what you already know, you're not looking for what you don't know or looking for an angle you haven't thought of. Rest assured, however, that your competitors are. At our last company, a guy came in asking to interview me and my brother. We were suspicious and wanted to know why this guy in wanted to interview us. Long story short, he told us that the big companies hired him to go in and find all the gaps in our company. Then they would go and write a contract that outdid ours. He told us that most business owners loved to talk about themselves and would usually tell him everything.

I thought, wow…what sabotage! But that's when I got the big picture. If you're not thinking of how your competitors are thinking, or wondering how people around you see things from a different viewpoint, then you're not making your best effort to succeed and provide a better service to your clients.

In the documentary *The Last Dance*, Michael Jordan noted in an interview that he wasn't working to be nice, he was working to win. If you want to be a champion, nice isn't the ultimate goal. He never said he wasn't nice, he said if he had to be seen as not nice, then fine. The confession brought him to tears. What I took out of that was that he was being empathetic; he was being kind. He saw potential in himself and others and did what was necessary to help achieve greatness. Being nice wouldn't have helped anyone win. He pointed out that you can't win against people who work as a team. He said he needed people around who challenged him; he made those team members better because they would challenge anything they didn't like. Steve Kerr was the perfect example; he challenged some of Jordan's behavior, didn't have any problem saying what he felt was being done wrong, and earned Jordan's respect along the way.

Kind Versus Nice Moving Forward

In the past, my business dealings have been negatively perceived as being too direct. Only later was my kindness applauded when it was finally recognized. As the pandemic progressed, I began to notice a change in tone and reception to kindness by our competitors and others having endured such horrors. Vendors, customers, partners, and many others have changed their perceptions during this pandemic and business appears to be evolving to a preference for kindness. There are many people who will go back to the way they were, but I would argue that they shouldn't. Kindness and empathy should be woven into all actions of doing business; those who support this way of interacting with others can watch how their revenues increase along with so many other benefits. I've worked with good people who are aligned with our mission, from vendors to CEOs and owners, many who basically were thinking this way already. Most of them want to save people a lot of time and money and frustration from dealing with others who don't think in the same way.

Those who have lived as though this way of conducting business with empathy and kindness plays second fiddle to the loud and self-centered executive will be forced to re-examine their positions on this if they want to lead effectively coming out of the pandemic. A leader would not show these traits in my opinion, nor will it suffice for the future. I think a new way of leadership will be demanded by team members: their leaders must act with empathy and kindness. Moving away from a mindset of doing business without empathy will only shed a positive light on your company. I have already tried to remove myself from dealing with that kind of negativity.

If anything, it seems that more customers and vendors have a deeper respect for me being like this. For instance, I took a $20,000 hit on a recent order because I wanted to save jobs. I couldn't act only for my interests; the pandemic wasn't the time for me to do something where so many people would lose their jobs because I didn't want to lose money on a deal. I told them, "Just ship it out, man." The guy said, "Man, they told me you was a good dude, but you crazy to lose this amount of money." He said, "You're all right by me, because I wouldn't have done that." He then told me, "Don't do that again."

Twenty years ago, people thought I was a dumb young kid that didn't know anything. Now there is weight to the way I do business. Living this way, and being successful, doesn't appear to be such a dumb idea or way of life. I have been told directly to my face, "I can't believe this works. I might need to look into why this is the case."

Entrepreneurship is taking a risk to make money. It's naïve to assume that I opened a for profit business to not earn income. This doesn't stop me and others from living a life and running a business that impacts others in a positive way.

This change in perception makes me feel good. I know that there are many people that are grateful for the way that I operate. When I wake up it is on my mind to make someone else's day. Whether it's a smile at a stop, or a kind word, the business arena needs people who treat others well. Not everyone I meet appreciates this. When I do come across someone that appreciates the way I do business, they know I'm experienced enough to know what I am doing and my actions and intentions are welcomed. They quickly learn that I want to do business, but I also want to make friends. I can do both and it's a way to make somebody's day.

People tend to forget that there's a human being on the other side of thc table who deserves kindness. They usually have similar, if not the same, issues you do—money, relationships, etc. You are unique as a human but no different than another person in deserving kindness and empathy from others. Everyone needs a smile; everyone needs to hear a good word. You have bad days, and they have bad days. And that's generally what you are dealing with. I work to find a way to ask "How are you doing today? What's going on?" that makes others feel better about themselves, life, me, and business.

Of course, you don't want to come across like you're crazy. You're not working to be best friends right off the bat. You want to just let others know you are interested in them. Let the relationship grow organically. It's that balance of "How you doing? I know, we have to engage and do business, but how are you doing?" What happens is that when you walk in like that, they're going to come with their best foot forward. They might think "I'm going to stick this guy for all his money," but they have made the wrong assumption. If that's the case, it's going to show, and I'll see it.

When this kind of attitude does show itself, if you have armed yourself with enough loyal people around you they're going to either help you find a competitor that can help or you're going to find a way to not use them just based on how they're interacting and responding to you. That's what happens when you start building value; you start making connections based on value. People who know who you will tell you if a vendor is not acting kind and will ask for help. People with wrong intentions won't realize the loyal following you might have. Yes, it takes time to get to that point, but you will quickly gain a following when you act like this.

Remember that a kind person will have a better chance at gathering more accurate intel about systems, processes, projects, or customers to effectively deliver solutions. They won't seek to be agreeable but rather view the motives and reasons for the actions or viewpoints needed to execute the mission at hand. They are truly thinking of the overall goal.

Many times those who lean towards being nice as a foundation will say yes when they mean no. Those who are kind in these situations often deal with positive outcomes from the recipients seeking their feedback. You never really know what a person is thinking. People are human and make mistakes and as a whole most are a bad judge of character. However, when you sense that someone is really working to do their best and their actions consistently mirror this then they develop a track record for showing that they can be trustworthy. You will only find this out once you have been dealing with them and have built a history together. People and firms evolve and empathy as a foundational block is not the standard yet. Only time will tell.

A company's true ethics are often revealed during a crisis or when a plan goes wrong. Hardship reveals true character; it is really the only way to find out about a person or a firm. We didn't seek immediate bids or orders to go after our first customer. We set an 18-to-24-month goal to secure our first customer. This allowed us to strategically focus on building the right connections for the right reasons. We took time to build relationships by learning what potential customers typically bought and when, what issues were going on at that time, who was buying, and who was the head lead. We found data on past customers. We learned how events had affected the way things were previously bought. Our approach is how we live, that includes taking care and showing real concern for all those involved in the buying process.

Taking the long approach was rocket fuel for our revenue once the foundation of our business was shown to be based on empathy. It was as if the flood gates opened for revenue. Our competitors were taking the short-term quick buys and in the same period when it looked like we weren't winning we were succeeding in building relationships. We would do this by helping some of our buyers find a better source, even if it wasn't us.

The nature of our business industry is that you have to position your product or service properly. We focused on helping. We helped bigger firms and perceived competitors. In doing this some of them took this as weakness and completely stayed off our trails on the customers and efforts we went after. It later turned out to be what solidified our business because it is now one of the many ways our customers buy now. In the process we learned who was loyal to us based on how they acted when we were helping them with no revenue. The relationships were built on a real desire to connect. Those who overlooked us at that time later came back to us asking to do business. In being kind, we offered to send them to other firms that might be helpful because our vendor base was already locked in.

Early on I was guilty of thinking that my empathetic ways were being taken as nice and agreeable. Outside advice said to reconsider and I chose to stay the course as we built trust and value. Sales are all about building value and trust; you can't build trust for the long haul if it's not based on authenticity. We would take deals at lower costs and we saw this as an opportunity to show the customers why we were the premier vendor. We planted our seeds in the buying cycles across the US and globally and by doing so focused on the long game. We may have been seen as nice until we were positioned with the deals and held the control on the buying vendors. In this role we were also able to show empathy and return kindness on the other end when it wasn't shown to us on the front end. In doing this we gained many previous vendors that were competitors and who soon became allies. We were able to cross outside commercial efforts that had no connection to us other than to provide goodwill to another firm to help them.

I had a vendor that was sent in to do our IT support. In doing this they missed the printing deadline we needed on a remote job. It took a last-minute call to a ground team that could do the printing job, kit it, and deliver it on the emergency timeline. It cost us an excessive amount of money not previously budgeted. In reaching back out to the initial vendor, I asked why they said yes if they couldn't do the work on time. They told me they were being nice, thinking they were helping me by taking on the work when they should not have. I then had to explain that it hurt us more than if they would have said no. In our line of business we survive on the ability of the supply chains to be empathic and kind to be able to express the truth in delivery time frames.

One of the biggest hurdles I specifically encounter is companies not understanding the weight and urgency of orders and the results when timelines aren't met. Nice won't help us succeed. Kind will because the kind firms are upfront and tell the truth. We have aligned our supply chain line with kind empathetic partners. We avoid nice.

You Are Not Weak

My experience in this domain was initially perceived by our competitors as weak and incapable. It was a miscalculation on their part. The customers saw our way of doing business as value added and welcomed it. By the time the competitors got wind of my movements, the relationships and work ethics were formed. Understanding people and how they think and respond will allow you to develop and execute a strategic plan that can be enacted. It will allow for a better chance at gaining intel and supporting your customers. This is the quiet warrior mentality. There's nothing weak about a kind person doing things for the betterment of others.

There is a consistent practice for many people to talk more about themselves and focus on the sale and not the value being delivered. This was not a habit of mine, and my lack of doing it often gave others the perception of me as a young, uneducated, non-threatening executive. At many industry events, other professionals overlooked me in conversations and blatantly spoke of insights into the projects being done. The reason I knew these were legit was because I studied the issues and projects myself to gain insight into the gaps within many of these firms. At 6'6', it is not difficult to find me in a public setting, which made the assumptions made about me even clearer.

Much is learned via observation and listening. The more you become skilled in empathy the more you are able to pick up on the energy being given off via the nonverbal cues from others.

I have been told directly to my face a few times that I don't belong in this space and that my company is nothing to be worried about. My strength was exercised in understanding this was their limited understanding of me. It didn't stop my desire to succeed or live with empathy and kindness. The desire to make genuine connections was usually received by subordinate team members at other firms who actually did the work and then ultimately became our allies.

These allies became strategic connections that kept my network strong and allowed me to build it quickly. Some of our most loyal customers were those who witnessed interactions at these events or who were relayed the responses I gave in these situations. Many would later voice how they saw my genuine kindness as refreshing and needed. It was another mental boost for me to continue living a life based on empathy and kindness knowing it would eventually pay off in both monetary value and goodwill to others.

At the company's core, we love to connect with and help others. It drives everything we do. Our mission is based on ensuring safety for others and playing a part in returning priceless cargo home to others. Empathy is the foundational block for our mission and our purpose doesn't waver due to others not understanding this way of living. Building long-term relationships matter to us because we know ultimately they may be part of saving someone's life one day by calling in an order or making a last-minute connection to save a project. I feel the perception is beginning to move towards others slowly seeing that kindness is a strength, and that business is better when it is widely practiced.

This way of doing business is effective and helped me to redirect a massive deal from a very large and well-known firm. It took research and strategy to win their trust. Understanding the mindset of the key players and their assumptions made at these events was critical for me to capitalize on their behavior towards me. It could be seen that they were speaking this way to throw me off, but my research said otherwise and their blatant disregard and lack of respect for me proved this. Armed with data, personalities, and assumptions it was one of the largest deals we secured in the company's existence.

It's not worth overlooking others because they do not fit the stereotypical mold of the loud, overly confident executive. It's the calm, well-spoken person I look for in these settings. Kindness is a different frequency. Those who are high in emotional intelligence, keen on empathy, and wise are tuned in to it. It doesn't take much to tune into its frequency; many times, it simply requires an open heart and a willingness to listen. Traveling on this frequency in business is like playing both offense and defense at the time same. It makes it difficult for others to fight you and it increases your chances for overall success at the same time.

CHAPTER 3

SEEKING SUCCESS WHILE PRIORITIZ-ING EMPATHY

Many people find it difficult to practice empathy while striving for success because they either don't understand its application or they fear being seen as weak.

Empathetic Grit

Being determined to live life and conduct business with empathy and succeed is what I call empathetic grit. Grit is defined as courage, resolve, and strength of character; empathy is defined as the ability to understand and share the feelings of another. Those who have empathetic grit have often endured many difficult trials in life and business that allow them to combine the two and apply them with military precision. Having developed the concept through struggles is not always the case, however. I have found in my experience that some naturally understand the importance or are born with the gift of being an empath. If being empathetic is not who you already are, you would be wise to learn how to become more empathetic to improve your ability to make deep connections with others. Some feel they have to be one way in business and another way outside of the boardroom. If being consistently empathetic is something you have difficulty applying or understanding, it may not click with you until you go through something extremely difficult that changes your position and understanding. Difficult experiences usually allow for one to manage, mirror, and show genuine empathy.

Empathy has caused many to shift and change when it has been applied to them or witnessed. It is a powerful force. I have seen vendors change their positions on projects and general conduct after encountering something tragic in their personal lives or business. These events noticeably changed their method of thinking, and their actions became more empathetic over time. Many I have seen this happen to have sustained this way of living in both their personal and professional lives. Some voiced that tragedies opened their eyes, and now living a life committed to listening and hearing others to understand is the foundation for their business and life. Making money in business is an elementary concept that business professionals understand. How we interact with others matters, however.

We had a former employee whose life brought about change. Their intentions were rooted in the right place, and lack of corporate experience was a teachable moment to show the importance of actions. Their kindness in being direct was an exceptional quality. In sitting with them during a revenue call and email follow-up, I had to point out that the tone of their voice and infrequent pauses were possibly seen as aggressive even though they meant well. When I showed them, there was an immediate awareness, and change occurred immediately. They stated their position in life was not wanting to be on the receiving end of this feeling. This was a simple training technique that only enhanced the core of the kindhearted person they were. Sometimes it only takes someone to point out an issue for the individual to truly learn how to be a better person and professional. This person has now quickly risen in their respective field, and it makes me very proud to see them make an impact on others' lives due to something I helped them learn. Empathy is now practiced in their life, and in their work domain. They are now on a trajectory to become a top executive in their industry. They may not have originally identified empathy as simple tones and word placements in emails; the revelation was eye-opening for them. In general, I feel many know they need to be kind; sometimes, it just has to be pointed out how this can be accomplished through actions. This employee has lived through tough times and was made aware of simple tweaks that have greatly improved their interactions with others.

The world needs more people who are quiet warriors built with empathetic grit. When leaders can show others how to tweak their actions to better themselves and others and direct them on a path for showing mastery in empathy, business interaction will only benefit. In business, moncy is exchanged for value or the perception of value. This process should include the intangible value of showing empathy. It has been proven to increase profits for revenue teams. I believe this is a byproduct of the actions of those high in cognitive and compassionate empathy. Those in the future will demand empathy from their leaders.

With grit and empathy combined, the best leaders focus on making an impact on others instead of just generating revenue. It goes deeper than monetary values. They are driven by purpose and impact. This framework places the context of the conversation in a different light. They are aware of their employees who have tough home situations to deal with and make accommodations for them in ensuring the office space is a safe zone to bring value and goodwill to them. They also understand that some of their employees are only there for a job to prepare them for their next goal. They lift these individuals up and work to help them as they build their skills to move forward along their personal paths.

Those who show grit in not giving up despite difficult circumstances often find themselves in situations which allow them to connect on a deeper level with others. These connections can help them overcome their situations and also teach them to live better lives through empathy and kindness. When I was at my most trying times, the deepest heartfelt connections were often facilitated by others through cognitive and compassionate empathy. The emotional empathy made the touchpoint. This also a two-sided coin in the application. When reaching out for help or expressing a need, lean in with emotional empathy and focus heavily on the cognitive application of empathy; this approach allows the other person or team to sense the emotion, make a cognitive decision, and respond in compassionate empathy. Approach a vendor or customer with this empathetic grit, and usually there will be a positive response to its application. It may cause a chain reaction in your business interactions and support your efforts to become (what I call) a logistician for humanity.

Empathetic Grit in Practice

Difficult decisions will adversely affect others no matter how much is done to prevent them. People will be let go, vendor changes or customer changes in buying will reduce revenue. Things will happen that will test the determination of pursuing important goals. The application of empathetic grit will focus on the long-term goal by addressing with cognitive empathy what is needed in the short term to address the immediate need. Compassionate empathy comes into play here and will deliver the tough decision with compassion to the affected people. This will help create an understanding of what really was the reason for the action.

Very large firms may benefit from taking this approach when they make decisions that affect others. In simple terms, some level of decency in communication may go a long way during very difficult decisions. Employees usually do better when they sense the care being given by leadership and the company. For example, if you need to downsize, it would be empathetic grit to ensure that most of your team stays employed. Cutting costs to delay the downsize for as long as possible is what many firms do before making the call to do it. Compassion in delivery may alert those teams that a possible downsize is coming if circumstances don't change. This allows others to prepare if you go ahead and get the people that you're downsizing other jobs. You go above the norm for your people if you can give everyone a severance package. I'm talking about large companies, like those that let 8,000 people go because they're changing over to software that's ultimately going to get the company into a more efficient realm and sustain the other 15,000 employees. What are you going to do for those you have to let go? Are you helping them get hired somewhere else? You're not likely to be able to get all of them other jobs, but what kind of assistance are you making to that end?

The late great Kobe Bryant was well known for his "mamba mentality," a relentless focus on constant self-improvement. Being relentless in applying empathy in business and having the grit to finish the identified purpose of the business or goal will yield significant results. Kobe focused on fundamentals and then built upon them. He said, "To sum up what mamba mentality is, it means to be able to work to be the best version of yourself constantly. That is what the mentality is. It's a constant quest to work to be better today than you were yesterday." This is something that those in business or seeking to reach a goal can do and make an impact. Have a "mamba mentality" and live it out with "empathetic grit."

Kobe's mamba mentality was part of why he was on the Los Angeles Lakers for twenty seasons. It was part of why he was feared on the court and won so many championship rings. He did the things others thought were unnecessary or "weak." When game time came, he was locked in and knew how to combat his opponents; he took focus to another level. His grit was shown in his determination. Cognitive empathy was applied in his actions, knowing who surrounded him, and he had compassionate empathy in delivery. The perception of how he did this may have been misunderstood, like Jordan in his documentary. Taking this example and applying it to business, a focus on empathetic grit to deliver excellence to others is worthy of practice and implementation.

A reporter once walked into a gym early to get ready for the day and saw Kobe practicing fundamentals. Kobe tied his mastery and elite abilities to the way he practiced fundamentals. Similarly, practicing the fundamentals of how to be compassionate and empathetic in business interactions will set a business up for great success.

When you reach a certain level of success, you're going to have to make hard decisions. If you have a reputation for being empathic and kind, people will be more likely to understand that the decisions were tough for you to make; they may not be happy about them, but they will be understanding. They will know that you are a person of true character and integrity, someone who understands how to operate as a true leader in a tough business world.

There was a time in my previous company when I was responsible for releasing team members. It was a very difficult task and one I took personally. I did my best to ensure we found jobs for them. I did not benefit from doing that, other than doing the moral thing and showing compassionate empathy during the process.

When I started KUOG Corporation, our company was part of a critical project. The vendor made a typo on their pricing to us and it was only identified after the urgent planning schedule was in place. Stopping the order would have caused massive disruption across the board, and lives were at stake. There was no time to change the project schedule, nor was the supplier, a large business, willing to change and adjust price because they had to answer to their shareholders. Being empathetic is not always going to achieve the desired outcomes. My company took a $50,000 hit. When the customer was made aware of what I did to help them save this project, I was immediately thanked. The benefits came later when other opportunities came our way as a result of our actions on this contract. My business started $50,000 in the hole.

Sound advice said not to follow through with the order. The purpose of ensuring safety overrode that option and, in hindsight, was a very wise decision for the revenue generated afterwards. My plan wasn't considered a success to me personally until our ten-year goal was reached. I expected bumps in the road, but not right out of the gate. It certainly was a trying time for me. The customer advised me that the order needed to be delivered and that lives were in danger if it wasn't completed as executed.

I asked myself, "Is somebody's life really worth that?" I knew that over time, I could make the money back. After a cognitive assessment of the situation, I responded with compassion. I delivered the order as promised and, in doing so, let them know I would make this back up over time. To me, lives were more important than the money, and that was non-negotiable. A lesson was learned about the vendor I worked with, and later I utilized the error to benefit me on another project. I have been told on many occasions that other people would not have done what I did. That's okay. It's not the first time I've been told that something I did was unwise. The same people who told me my actions were unwise also became my allies for critical support on future projects.

Determination and Compassion

I was determined to always be compassionate in my communication with others. I experienced the power of how effective it was numerous times. A company's weakest link may be the person who is overlooked. It is wise for companies to take the way team members are treated seriously. Most will not alert the company of a plan to exit. It's human nature to want to be treated with respect and value. Hire based on kindness and ensure the culture supports this so that the investments made in talent aren't wasted when people leave based on poor support in moral actions. Creating a company culture of collaboration, safety, and empathy will go a long way toward rctaining quality employees and is its own defense against competitors. Tolerance to those who ignore compassion and empathy is not suited for vibrant work cultures. Draw a line in the sand, show more empathy in actions, and require this from leadership. It is good for business, customers, and your team members. Cognitive empathy is the basis for the best solutions in the workplace. The suggestion here is that a little bit of compassionate empathy goes a long way. Overriding cognitive solutions with compassionate empathy doesn't benefit and will reduce profits if decisions are made solely on emotional empathy. Compassionate empathy is dealing with how information is delivered and shared. This is an important focus. Leaders benefit by asking, "Do I lack a certain amount of compassion?" or "Am I showing too much compassion?" There needs to be an appropriate balance. Sadly, the lean is towards not showing enough compassion.

It requires high proficiency in cognitive empathy to show compassionate empathy. Some of the questions raised will be thoughts about how decisions will impact everyone involved. How will it affect those that may not be happy about the decision? How will I temper those who benefit and respond to those on the team who don't? If I were on the receiving end of this news, how would I be feeling? Being direct, with kindness, is being compassionate. There is a misconception that one must be mushy and soft when delivering disappointing news. It is the opposite. What's most important is being mindful of the feelings of others while presenting information and showing care in your responses to their questions and concerns. You may have one person or a group of people that you have to deal with; either way, you have to consider the best way to deal with each situation empathetically. Overall, your goal is to make it clear that you understand how others feel. You need to clarify that for the company, this is how we're going to roll. Let them know you are honestly engaging with them to get opinions or to hear them speak about the situation.

In my experience, I have seen where the tendency is to go from one extreme to the other; for example, executives that were too harsh move to becoming too lenient. There is usually a red flag shown by the one in a leadership role seeking to please the masses instead of making cognitively empathetic decisions that benefit others. Narrowly focusing on being compassionate to conduct business is counterproductive. It places a business in a position to pull back on the determination to push the envelope when it needs to. Utilize compassion to push the envelope when the situation calls for it. Apply the different domains based on the emotions presented as if playing a chess game.

Winning at All Costs is Losing

Monetary success at all costs, inclusive of pain to others, is a losing formula. In the end, the realization comes when many are solo in their success or at their death bed alone. Money is a tool. In the hands of those with the morals and motives to help others, it is impactful. I am an advocate for success with money so that others can benefit. Succeed in the right way with foundations built on empathy. Leverage the successes in life to assist others who may not have been afforded the opportunities you've worked for or been given. This is my definition of winning.

Thinking long-term about the domino effects of decisions, businesses would be wise to consider outside of the numbers what impact is being made to assist others along the way for their betterment. What actions are being done today that will negatively affect the sustainment of humanity's social well-being?

The generally accepted definition of sustainability is the ability to be maintained at a certain rate or level. It is the avoidance of the depletion of natural resources in order to maintain an ecological balance. Our world is working to regain a hold on sustainability in partnership with business. Sustainability requires us all to do our part to bring about effective change and lasting results. Entrepreneurs and others play a critical role in leading the way to help this world deliver sustainable products, solutions, and actions that will leave this planet better for those left to carry the torch.

We all have the opportunity to be stewards of the Earth. How we educate our youth on utilization of resources and their responsibilities for the life they have been given matter. Leadership training focused on how to build leaders for tomorrow is wonderful when it produces what I call social responsibility warriors. These are professionals, educators, businesses, influencers, and most importantly, the grassroots teams doing the actual work in the areas needed to move this mission forward. In the derivative Latin, *sustinere* means to "hold up, hold upright; furnish with means of support; bear, undergo, endure." There are many ways that entrepreneurs can work to hold up, support, and assist in efforts for sustainability.

Now is the time to start working with firms who are working to make a difference; seek the help of those on the buying side to select products or solutions from preferred partners or products. More business needs to be driven towards firms with certifications in sustainability who are acting on bettering the planet. Partnerships—and an awareness of these companies—will help consumers seek out businesses that are socially, economically, and globally responsible to the Earth. Genuine actions will provide businesses with loyal brand customers who want to align themselves with businesses who support sustainability. Many awards now acknowledge the impact businesses and those who are doing good have on this world. These businesses who are making an impact on the world benefit from being rewarded with consumers who buy from them, partnerships who get behind them with the proper resources, and more media coverage on their successes for what they are doing both in business and sustainability.

Not all businesses can create products or solutions that fully embrace the complete adoption of sustainable practices, but they can begin to move in a direction that helps align them with programs, organizations, and companies who can and help them further the cause. Collaborating with successful teams will be rewarding and can help show others that success can be achieved through the execution of empathy.

Give Back to Where You Came From

Local communities benefit from empathetic leaders. These leaders realize the importance of social accountability. One of my favorite quotes is from John Bunyan, "You have not lived today until you have done something for someone who can never repay you." This is empathy at its core. Giving back is kindness. A leader may earn significant profits and, in the process, inspire fifteen others to create equal success. This skillful knowledge passed on to those who created this success is priceless and closely associated with empathetic actions.

Empathy isn't the silver bullet to all business growth. In standard business, there are two sides to a win: a monetary loss and gain. Both provide learning experiences, and neither lessen the importance of empathy being shown. Applying empathy on a losing side of monetary value may increase the chances of collaboration. When tough decisions have to be made, empathy helps with the perception that the actions were based on authenticity. The historical data of the action will prove how real the perception is. If an order needs to be delivered to ensure that fighters get back home, someone may want to make extra money on that order. If I feel that the purpose and reason for the order far outweighs the money being requested, I will take an order at a loss to make the solution possible.

Extreme Ownership

As previously mentioned, *Extreme Ownership* is a book that has been a really big influence on me. This book shows in action what mastery of empathy looks like via the concept of extreme ownership by leaders. Taking ownership as a leader is being empathetic. It is mastery in cognitive empathy. Navy SEALs endure some of the harshest situations yet have high success rates. They do this with lives at stake, the highest asset available to give. SEALs are determined and masters in team building. This takes empathy. I have yet to find someone who would reference a Navy SEAL as weak and a master of empathy. My encounters with them have shown that their ability to listen and understand are unparalleled. Their focus is on getting things done correctly the first time and they concentrate on building leaders and teams. The leadership training they receive is tested and proven in the most austere environments. It takes all domains of empathy to be a leader, in my opinion, in these situations. They have built an entire training focused on leadership.

I took from this book how empathy is needed to be an effective leader. Some may disagree. Navy SEAL teams are formulated from the best of the best recruits. These individuals are then trained to be excellent leaders by teaching them to own each situation. The authors give constant advice to executives who express fear in speaking to their own teams about change, usually a difficult circumstance for anyone. For the authors to speak to these executives about identified issues along with a path to execution in a manner that is received well takes empathy in all domains. It was striking to see a battle-tested warrior be the one to walk into an office setting and evoke change utilizing emotional, cognitive, and compassionate empathy. I already held our military in high regard before reading this book and gained an even deeper level of respect for them. I highly recommend the book to everyone.

A person who understands how to apply empathy gains great intel on those they interact with and can use it to help better them. For those who ignore this opportunity, they are missing out on the chance to capitalize on the situation. Showing empathy can only benefit the business and those who show it.

Leadership the Right Way and the Wrong Way

In a leadership role, the importance of the position is more than just the monetary benefits it might bring to a business; it is the intangibles that leave marks on the hearts of the others. When Dan Price was hiking with his friend Valerie near Seattle, he realized that her life was in trouble. Her rent had gone up $200, and she was struggling financially. He was angry; he knew she had served in the military for over a decade, had done two tours in Iraq, worked fifty hours a week at two jobs, and wasn't making it.

Price owned Gravity Payments, and he realized that his staff must also be struggling, so he decided to fix it. He immediately and significantly raised the salary at Gravity Payments for all his people. Price acted with empathy. He saw that the world was an unequal place, and as a millionaire, he realized he could do something about it.

Price is an excellent example of a leader showing how empathy can positively affect the lives of others. His decision to raise salaries showed strength and the path less traveled. His company ultimately benefited from these actions based on his genuine desire to help others. Leading with actions that touch the lives of team members goes a long way in building a solid company culture and increasing revenues. There is power in showing empathy. His company is doing better than ever as a result.

Positions of power should be held by people of high moral regard. Holding power in the right way is important. Today's youth are seeing the way leaders act, are taking a closer look at what companies stand for, and are making the decision to either align with them or steer their buying power somewhere else. The best thing that could happen is that companies lead for the right reasons. Since many need a monetary reason to act, this may be one worth entertaining. The consumer base may be moving towards companies that show kindness in their actions, that live up to the words they market and brand with. If those in leadership positions won't change to live this way because it's the right thing to do, then the consumer may soon force them to by way of their revenue reduction. Leadership based on empathy and kindness will always be in high demand.

A YouTube video called "What Is Privilege?" demonstrates the differences of context really well. Kids are lined up for a race and given directions like, "If you have both parents, step forward one step. If you have a good education, take another step." You see kids of different races at the starting line and, as the video continues, you see those of minority backgrounds fall behind; some never move. The narrator notes that some people are born into better circumstances.

When it is time to actually start the race, some participants are already at the finish line; some are halfway there, and some are still at the starting line. It's obvious that people come from different beginnings. It will take different methods to give everyone an equal chance. Showing compassion to the person at the finish will be different from how you show it to the ones in the middle and definitely to those who never left the starting line. This is where cognitive empathy is needed most in business. Understanding the business and the teams, compassionate empathy can be given proportionately to create a culture of cohesiveness. The emotions of team members from the back of the line versus those towards the front are simply different and require a fluid application of empathy to align with the purpose of the business. Showing empathy to increase the overall success of a company is being adaptive; fairness needs to be shown to others both collectively and individually. Making all team members happy is something to aspire to. In most cases, teams seek to ensure the application method is the same even if it varies in delivery. The same application should be made with empathy.

Why is Listening First Vital in Seeking Success While Prioritizing Empathy?

Listening is a critical pillar of empathy. Making your presence known by how others are left feeling after an encounter with you is priceless. It is the preferred way I choose to make my presence known, a quiet confidence that naturally engages others. This comes from listening and asking meaningful questions that allow for others to speak to what matters to them. In this way, they are speaking and sharing information to build on a good conversation. Learning usually takes place in these types of conversation that otherwise would have been missed when speaking more than listening happens. This method allows for a dialogue of thoughts versus sharing of statements. When a greeter at a restaurant shows no sign of compassion to the patrons that enter, it makes it difficult to assess if the team or establishment will treat its patrons fairly. The same goes for companies. Customer service teams who ignore these concepts and are the first touchpoints can turn away customers. No position is too large or too small; all will benefit from applying empathy in action—the small things matter. Make them count with empathy.

Nike was given a lesson in the harsh reality of what happens when this basic concept is not followed. Steph Curry was considering a deal with Nike. His meeting with the company directly followed Kevin Durant's meeting. The team he was meeting with hadn't bothered to prepare an exclusive presentation for Steph but were reusing the same presentation they had used for Kevin Durant. When Steph and his team walked into the room, Kevin Durant's name was on the screen. The Nike team addressed him as Stefan and this turned him off. It was a complete disregard for compassion and an overall lack of a basic understanding, on an emotional level, for addressing someone by their proper name. This showed a lack of cognitive understanding of being able to handle a shoe deal. How a person shows emotional and compassionate empathy is a good way to determine the prowess of cognitive empathy in the solution. It is extremely difficult to overcome this when there is a blatant disregard for emotional and compassionate empathy. The foundation for trust is off to a shaky start. Putting myself in his shoes, I would have walked as well. If they couldn't get the importance of a name right, I would have concerns for their ability to get something as simple as a shoe lace design correct. I might ask for a blue lace, they might overlook the request and send in a green one. This was certainly an extreme situation.

Nike showed they felt that Steph was second to Durant. Whatever the reason, the perception was not the best for Nike. The team working for Nike represented Nike in a less than stellar light. Nike lost out by not sending those high in emotional IQ and empathy to address Steph. Most know which shoe and brand Steph ultimately chose—Under Armour®. In this process, Nike lost immeasurable amounts of money. Their greatest loss, however, was the trust of a superstar whose name they couldn't get right.

I have learned to engage with people and allow them to speak. In critical situations, the exchange between people can happen quickly, and often is a way for one party to gain leverage over another. There are times the simple tone of the buyer or a contact's pause can tell of a gap in power. It can allow one to attack with cognitive empathy when the emotional cues are picked up. Those who play the game of being tough usually are the ones who have difficulty holding their emotions in check when empathy is applied.

It's human nature to make assumptions. To be set in them is a different way that usually does not respond well to cognitive empathy. It places a person in an unguarded position, and they become a sitting duck to those skilled in empathy. I have learned in these situations to sit back and listen. Making assumptions about people in business puts a massive target to be locked in and engaged with empathy. These assumptions have often been made about me, and I have been able to lock in with empathy in doing so. I use this method because, at my core, I am driven to learn from others and build deep relationships. It is usually when I encounter this that others see me seeking to do this for ulterior motives.

As an introvert and empath, initial connections can be quite draining because I sense the energy deeply from those making these assumptions. Empathy is a tool that helps me function in a business setting to overcome this introversion. When I show this to others, this works, and the response seen from it being applied is joyous. In general, I have found that people enjoy talking about what matters deeply to them. Find this touchpoint, and it will provide an opportunity for you to engage in communication with empathy. This is why listening is so important. Whenever another person provides a window into their soul, be sure to lend an open ear. It is a way they may be testing your ability to listen and solve an issue. Taking this approach can be seen by others as weak and leave you open for them to perceive it as an advantage against you. It is an assumption. It is the equivalent of putting hands down against a prized champion fighter in a heavyweight fight—exposure to an attack with empathy.

When others make assumptions, it is usually accompanied by letting their guard down. There is a tendency to view those that act in empathy as non-threatening and lacking in intelligence. Information begins to flow freely in situations that are not suitable for dissemination. Those wise to understand empathy pick up on these missteps and leverage them to benefit their own missions. Lessons are learned in these settings about the character of others that later can become entry points to a business competitor that is not taking care of its team.

Plato was quoted as saying, "Wise men speak because they have something to say; fools because they have to say something." This speaks to how others view empathy in most settings. When it's clear that assumptions have been made in situations, allow the other to continue to speak. The continuance of information provided will be a wealth of data to support when speaking toward their teams or as leverage to secure new work. Calling others foolish for speaking is not the intent here. It references how I handle myself in the situations I find myself in when assumptions are placed on me. The more others speak in my presence, the more I learn. When I finally speak, it is based on the strategic execution of my plan.

It's difficult to help others when listening to them is problematic. It is the medium by which the most information is presented to allow for mastery in cognitive empathy. Compassionate and cognitive empathy are skills that work best when they mirror buying and sales cycles. It will help solidify the revenue teams grasp on customers by the deep connections made and show mastery in empathy.

Many of my relationships developed by simply listening to someone and showing a sincere interest in what they were saying. I secured a large order this way. The point of contact was eventually moving to the firm that would support me on the massive deal. It was not known to me then. This point of contact shared with me that the initial part I asked for was good but had a better recommendation. The way they explained this to me, I could tell the knowledge base was vast. I asked them what sparked their interest in this field. They went on to explain a wonderful story of how a parent started their love for the industry. They continued gaining as much education in the process. The current location was not recognizing their worth. It was a long conversation, and pleasantries were exchanged.

A few days later, I dropped by the location to thank this person face to face, and the joy that radiated from them further confirmed that this would be a person I would want to work with in the future. When they informed me of the new location they were going to, I confirmed that we would buy the deal we had pending from them. Their excellence in the industry helped me deal with a critical order that needed to be delivered, and their best friend was an executive at another firm that was able to help me get the order out with a phone call from their friend. They became our closest confidant to this day. It all started from being deeply interested in them.

Dale Carnegie's book *How to Win Friends and Influence People* shows the importance of paying attention to the small details in human interaction. The book was relevant when first published in 1936, and it's relevant now. It does not take much to show interest in others, and the benefits for doing so may place a firm on a trajectory toward massive success.

CHAPTER 4

REVENUE GROWTH, SUSTAINMENT, AND COMPASSION

Sustainment is Built on Pillars of Compassion

Compassion and revenue growth have a unique connection. Many may ask, "How does that work?" During your revenue growth, the founders, teams, and executives typically are engaged to build a strong foundation for the business. There is a shift going on as we move through this pandemic towards leaders reevaluating their ability to build with empathy and show compassion while also growing and sustaining a business. A deep focus on heart-centered connections with your teams and customers is a path that can lead to extraordinary success if it is genuine.

Actively listen to the people you seek to help and then utilize compassionate empathy to relay your cognitive understanding of what you have heard. This is cognitive empathy done well. Compassionate empathy is what helped me grow quickly and forge deep relationships. It is how I personally see the future moving towards businesses and leaders who understand this well and apply it. For new business selling value, you have to hear and understand your customers. This is rooted in being highly proficient in cognitive empathy. In short order, it takes seeing the situation from their standpoint and leveraging the emotional cues you pick up in conversation with emotional empathy.

Businesses can grow on foundations not built on empathy and compassion. They may even achieve all they desired when starting out. In my opinion, along with the experience I have seen, these types of companies may find it difficult to be as equally impactful as those whose foundation and sustainment are built with empathy while continuing to deliver compassion in growth and sustainment. The impact made beyond the monetary exchange will be lasting and breed deep loyalty against your competitors. This method was highly successful for me, and I believe large and small firms can have great success this way as well. It is a differentiator. The digital age is here, and somehow you will need to stand out over others; doing this based on real care and compassion is an impactful way to do it. A passion for showing compassion in business drove my actions to match what was being said and aligned with our mission. Growth is sometimes uncomfortable yet necessary for success. Leading this way and building on compassion benefits those you serve as well as your revenue. Your methods and processes for handling growth may change, but the premise for growing with empathy and compassion at its core won't.

Growing while practicing moral decision making is an effective strategy. The strategy is based on a foundation of delivering compassion in communication, making deep connections with knowing when and how to utilize all the domains of empathy. Work in the now to help others and be compassionate at whatever level you are at.

Actions need to be practiced now. I found in my interactions that money and success reveal who you are at your core. If you are kind before money, you are more likely to be kind after obtaining monetary wealth and success. Those who find it difficult to build on empathy and transparency when wealth is achieved may find that the character adjustment to show compassion to the plights of others may be out of reach for them to comprehend and act on.

The quiet warrior is a concept I live by and I seek out others who live in this same manner. They move through the business sector by actions, not just words. These individuals are usually neurodiverse and have a deep curiosity for many things outside of their own field. Being the loud voice in the room is not something they will usually be known for. Mistaking them for being incapable of doing this when needed is a flaw as well. They have developed a skill for connection and how to hear others by a natural way of engaging. If you are curious about another field, you have to understand their positions on subjects fully. If this becomes a habit for you, the skills practiced will be useful in your daily interactions in your own line of work. This practice will help strengthen your soft skills and is an exercise in empathy.

How Do Revenue Growth and Compassion Connect?

In my experience, I have found that revenue growth and compassion are deeply connected as you shouldn't seek to have one without the other. If you're selling value, then you have to understand what you're selling to bring value. You have to have compassion and empathy to understand that, and if you don't have it, you're building a house on sand.

Some people can do it, but in my opinion, in my own experience, that's not what helped me get to the revenue levels achieved by the firms I have owned. Being a quiet warrior with an arsenal of emotional, cognitive, and compassionate empathy as my tools is what my foundation was made from.

High-dollar value contracts and deals are based on trust in most cases. This is formed by excellence in cognitive empathy delivered with flawless compassion to touch on the emotional state of others—in short, building a good friendship. In my case, returning our military personnel home safely after being on the other end of having a brother in a similar situation was my passion. Money only funded the continued effort to ensure we were a major supplier in a line helping others get safely home. To be in this work, it was normal for me to feel a supplier should have compassion for the soldiers that are out there as well as the parents and family members of those going to war. It would be naïve of me to think that supplying materials would get everyone home. It is always before me that the material may not save lives, but helping them have enough of it to have a better chance of survival matters deeply to me. If all we cared about was the dollar, the directives to our teams would be to make as much as possible on every order, but that's not how we set out to build the company.

Many would say the opposite, that compassion causes a lack of growth because you're not as cutthroat as other people. But that's not true. I believe that cognitive empathy increases profit margins. This is not by design; rather, the nature of your teams who understand this is that the value that needs to be delivered and they utilize compassion to support both the company and customer in a win-win situation. As you grow, you are growing in a sustainable, tactical way. The clients and customers you take on will often allow you to impact them with compassionate empathy. You will leave them an intangible deposit to their soul for the kindness you show them. It is certainly true that you're not going to take on a client that consistently makes things extremely difficult for you; you will also not want to work with those that blatantly set out to harm you or that you don't believe in or who you don't believe you can help.

As previously noted, Warren Buffett says his success came because he learned to say no. Just because somebody brings you a lucrative contract doesn't mean it aligns with your overall success. You already know you're not going to work with a customer you don't believe you can help. This is an efficient application in cognitive empathy. How you support, select, and refer others is a practice in compassionate empathy. You're taking the approach of selecting who your customer is by using empathy and helping them whether they see it or not.

You saying "no" could be the very thing that you need to do. It's something I haven't always been good at. Speaking frankly, the early tendency is to secure work at all costs to build momentum. Building connections deeply rooted in a genuine framework may be the reason you pass on other opportunities. Suppose you have identified via your business plan those customers you are working to attract. In that case, the connections you create by offering your support during your building years may be the very ones that help you land the larger deals. This is not a new concept, and one I feel is often overlooked. Wise executives with reach may be able to inquire from your early connections and match them against your current actions with them to assess the authenticity of your motives.

When you build a reputation for being a firm based on empathy and morality, it allows you to be in the driver's seat with your vendor selections. Who you pick helps further the cohesion of your partners to your purpose and how your honor your commitments to your customers. Compassion will help you grow by the communication in reactions when things don't go your way. It is telling in these situations for the characters of the people you are dealing with. It's a preview of how they may act in a situation if you work them and something doesn't go as planned; they are showing subtle signs, so handle them with care.

You're going to have to engage in compassion; you're going to have to consider that people are home with their kids, that they've got other things going on. You're going to have to consider what social media is saying. All these things now matter because interactions are no longer limited to walking into a room and being able to assess personal and social cues via the presence in the room.

You should be building your foundation on compassion; you need to be mindful of those who knowingly have no concern for others and who purposely seek to harm them. The business world in general is now moving towards a foundation built on compassion; since this is how I've always been, it's nice to hear others talking about that right now. Being on the Clubhouse app is showing me that many people are aligning with and confirming this way of doing business.

Sustainment is Directly Connected to a Business Model

Things go wrong in business. Unforeseen issues can occur quickly without time to adapt in the manner you would normally like. Character strength and soft skills will be even more critical for the future. People went into 2020 thinking they were going to have their greatest year, and they didn't. That means people being released and losing their jobs. When compassion, empathy, and genuineness in actions are known from your customers, vendors, and employees, it lessens the blow to the difficult decisions that must be made in business settings to ensure others can survive.

It can be a catch-22. Someone is going to have to lose out in certain situations for others to make it. It's going to come across a lot different for your vendors, customers, and people when they know you mean well at heart. These situations will be difficult if you, your teams, and your company have not shown compassion. A business will have a greater chance for sustainment and attract talent that wants to align with its mission when it shows compassion in its endeavors.

Many successful people often ask those aspiring to next-level success, "What's your purpose?" "What's your mission?" There comes a point when a certain level of revenue is reached, and momentum is moving in your favor, that the intangibles of your character are deciding factors for how business will be secured. Others at this level are looking to see if your moral beliefs and business mission are in alignment. They ask, "What is it that is driving that company? What is their mission? What are they doing that I can align myself and get behind?" This shouldn't be taken personally and gets back to what Warren Buffett talks about in terms of being able to say no. Your actions can place you in the presence of those who would otherwise not work with you based on your position, but because of the level of empathy and compassion you have shown, they will. They will respect that you have shown empathy and not bend to the ways of their beliefs. Your compassion may touch them and, in turn, build a strong ally.

People want to align with companies that show compassion and empathy from the top down. Think about how Google and other businesses acted when the pandemic hit. They showed cognitive empathy for the emotions of their teams and showed compassion in allowing their teams to work from home. Many others followed suit. They were at the top of many "where to get a job" lists during the pandemic for this reason and added to their talent pool. There was an influx of people asking, "How can I go there and get a job?"

When you have compassionate leaders who live their missions through their actions, people want to align with them. People don't want to work with or for a company that's not compassionate. Most are not telling themselves, "Oh yeah, I want to go work there."

It seems the world, in general, has had an awakening. If anything good has come out of the pandemic, I would say that it has caused many to seek a massive change in how leaders and companies should conduct business. In my opinion, there are two sides of the coin on this; you either want to live and make a conscientious effort to live based on your connections in empathy, or you're going to continue as if empathy has no place in life, especially the business setting. Whatever's going on, this new era is pointing to one of those two sides, so look at the side you most align with. I believe that empathy in action will emerge as a critical pillar for success.

I saw a post from Jocko Willink in the early months of 2021. He noted one of the biggest mistakes he sees leaders make: they don't own up to it when they make an error. And they're fearful about their bosses, "Oh, I made a mistake, what's he going to do?" He mentioned how one of the biggest things you can do as a leader is own your mistake and say, "Look, I messed up, I'll change." That's empathy, that's owning the situation.

Building Based on Moral Decision Making

This section is geared towards younger people and those looking for a fresh start, maybe after the pandemic, or at the beginning of a new venture.

When you start a business, you are starting to build your foundation. Many people get into business and start out right away saying, "I have a new business; how do I grow it?" You have to think, when you start your business, is it ready? Don't just jump into it; take your time.

You're going to have to go to different events; you're likely going to have to give out free advice. You should come across so that people know they genuinely matter. This may mean running into a flower shop and saying, "Good afternoon, is there something I could do to help?" It has no relation to your business, you have maybe made a mark with a flower shop owner, and somebody comes in who is involved in your business. They pass the referral, saying, "Hey, have you checked this kid out?"

Everything you do strategic wise, whether it's in your domain or not, do it widely. This can be wherever you are, volunteering, going out and offering free advice or help, helping a vendor, or something that lays a seed. As you become more successful, align yourself with programs and missions. If you see a need or a disaster, go and offer to help.

You're doing things that may not have a monetary value now, but you're building a wide net of people seeing you genuinely working to help. In doing that, you're not thinking about revenue in the immediate sense. If you're just starting out, then you're doing stuff at your level to make an impact. At every level, make an impact for social good. By doing that, you're setting yourself up to move to the next level.

Base your life and your business on doing good for others when it doesn't benefit you so that when you are in a position that it does, it will be second nature for your actions. The "optics" may say differently; the people and those who know you will support it as deserving for what they know you are doing. Do unto others how you want to be treated. No small act is ever wasted when kindness is involved.

The Quiet Warrior

You have two ears and one mouth. Temper the notion to speak above others; shut up and listen. You learn much by letting other people talk. Being a quiet warrior means you're sitting down and you're learning because when you finally do go on the attack, you basically have hit every pressure point.

There is no defense when you go on the attack, and by attack, I mean you deploy every tool at your disposal to touch a person's heart. You use every skill you have to make somebody leave feeling better for having interacted with you.

You are a quiet warrior because you're sitting back listening to everything they want to say. If they had a bad day, and they are unloading on you, it's OK. Seek to view from their position, and you may say to yourself, "OK, this person just told me everything I need to know, so I'm going to deploy every act of kindness, every reason why they've just told me it wouldn't work, and fill the gaps."

The quiet warrior is a valuable team member. These are the people that do things quietly behind the scenes, not looking for any rewards; they just do things because it is the right thing to do. These are your workers who will give help, give advice, your vendors who go out of their way to work to do the right thing and make the right connections.

If you're an executive, the title of quiet warrior should not make you complacent if you have a successful business. You should act as if it's your first day. You should never lose that curiosity for others, that quietness to sit and understand where people are, whether they're your employees or your vendors.

A quiet warrior is skilled in reading non-verbal actions and listens to people while viewing responses from their vantage point. Compassion should be the foundational character trait in the C of C-suite. You never become so high up on the totem pole that you cannot learn from others who don't share the same level of financial success. Learn to listen. Be the executive who values hearing from the janitor as much as they do their executive teams.

The premise of me saying this speaks to showing compassion to others; you never know where life has taken people. In college, my friend I were walking through the inner city of Atlanta. At the time, a homeless man crossed our paths asking for food. My friend thought it was funny to laugh and tell him to go away. The man seemed full of positive energy, and I proceeded to ask him how he was doing on such a cool night. It sparked a conversation. He spoke with clarity as though he was Ivy educated. As we went back and forth, I asked at some point if he had a place to go. He said he would be OK and that I reminded him of his son that he doesn't see because he lost everything. It turned out he was a successful professional athlete who played when I was a newborn. It left a mark on me that most people are not far from being homeless as the result of a few bad decisions.

I had enough to give him $5 to get something at the Waffle House. He thanked me for stopping to show this kindness and said it was a quality to carry on in my life. It marked me to see someone who had a successful run in the high points of life reach a low and appreciate such a kind act. He said that had been one of his greatest skills in the locker room to "own" space, and it was an effective way to lead and interact with others. All people have something to share, and you may find out something interesting just by listening to them. That situation taught me how to engage and speak to someone as an equal, forgetting about their circumstances. It allowed me to view myself as homeless and appreciate having someone speak to me with kindness and not pity. He taught me to become a lifelong learner from others.

A billionaire I knew left a massive impact on me. I thought someone at his level would do things differently. He was 100 percent the very essence of a quiet warrior. This guy was curious about everything and would listen before he spoke. He told me that's how he made his meteoric rise. He said what he wanted to say, he meant what he said, and he did what he said he would do. He was an approachable billionaire, and considered a kind executive by all who knew him. He was not weak; he was not soft. He was a quiet guy and one of the most powerful people I know.

I had an epiphany and told myself that this lifestyle could work. No one can ever tell me that being kind and empathetic cannot work because here's someone who did it, and did it at that level.

Say No the Right Way

It is vital to learn how to say no to requests and demands on your time while still being respectful. There are ways to tell people no without being rude.

There are two kinds of no. The one I call the hard no means being immovable because it's tied to a moral purpose. The solution no, however, means no because this should be rethought in order to formulate a better idea. No can mean either come back with a better idea or your values can't be bought. Either they're going to leave it alone, or they will deal, or they're going to come back with a better reason for showing you why something works and how it aligns with your goal. If you don't want a product, if you feel like it's going to dump oil in a river or something like that and you don't like it, you're saying, "I don't care how much money you're giving, I'm not going to take the deal, because I'm not tearing up the environment."

If they come back, you want to tell them, "Look, I really like the product, I really feel aligned with this, but I'm not doing it because it's not worth the money." If they're wise, they're going to come back and say, "What can we do to assure you that this is not going to be done?" You're likely to start having conversations, which may open up to other things that speak to show you're living your morals. You are crossing the line into a deeper relationship with them; whether they align with you or not, you showed a vulnerable side to allow for a connection. This is why it is important to begin saying no in alignment with your values as early as possible; you do not want to feel like you are doing trial and error on the biggest deal of your life.

They may not do a deal with you, but they may refer and connect you with somebody who says, "Hey, look, they're doing something similar to what you are; maybe this can help." Stuff comes out of saying no when you're showing empathy in that regard. Your no can eventually turn into another opportunity. It seems to me you eventually circle back around to the same people. It may not be today, but when you're in your industry long enough, you run back into the same people.

For example, maybe you have a vendor who wants to switch a military vest in an order for 100,000 of the vests. You know, without a shadow of a doubt, that that material is going to put warfighters in harm's way, but it's ten cents cheaper. That's a no. Ten cents for a life is not worth it.

They could come back and say, "Well, look, the next option is ten cents more which will reduce your overall profit." I can say thanks, or I can say no, we will not sacrifice safety for that. Maybe some time down the road, we can reengage this conversation when your specs meet the safety specs to ensure these individual's safety.

The True Path to Revenue

Many people focus on shortcuts because they don't want to do the work. They don't want to put in the time it takes to build a relationship and real value. Their mindset is different. They want rewards without sacrifice or work. They want revenue without connection. This is a generalization made from the interactions I see daily in business. The other way is, "Let me be valuable, let me bring value, let me learn and understand you so I can know what makes you tick." You'll learn more about what they don't like than what they do like.

It's not always about what they like; it may be what they don't like. You will have to always pay attention to new products and services that add value and benefit. Business is like dating. If you are looking for the one you plan to build a long-term relationship with, you will approach them differently. Your intentions from the start are usually going to be based on ensuring you can build a foundation for a long-term relationship. Your customers, vendors, and teams are those who you are looking to keep for a long time. Short-term flings in dating can cause a lifetime of pain, and picking the right partner in a marriage can build a lifetime of memories. The same goes for business; what is the purpose for your actions and engagements?

To connect with someone, you have to show deep interest in them. Inquire about the things that matter to them. In the dating example, in courting them, you're going to want to know their favorite colors. Are they morning or night people, do they like to travel, or what do they like to do for fun? Signs of omission may tell as much as what they say. Listening is critical. Ask questions. I have found that when you really show you care, people want to talk to you.

Many people want short-term gains, and they don't want to do the work. Entrepreneurship takes time. Our goal is to gain customers we want to service and maintain a relationship with for life. It's a different approach. Interactions are conversations. We view this as a mutual relationship. It is certainly common that most in business feel they want this. We really want a business relationship that extends past the transaction.

I don't want a customer that's just a number. I want you to interact with us because you want to be here; you see the value as much as I see the value. It's a mutual relationship. Some customers do simply want to buy with no real engagement, which should not stop you from still showing care in all your interactions.

It took our first company eighteen months to get an order. The second company took about the same time. If you're the typical person starting out, budget two to three years. This is the standard recommendation, and from my experience going all in, it is quite accurate. With the digital transformation going on, you may get there sooner, and that's always a plus to get there ahead of schedule. Stop thinking you're going to be successful in three or four months. That's just not realistic. It may happen to some people, but those are usually well connected, wealthy individuals.

The true path to revenue focuses on the long term by forging relationships built on trust and loyalty. My advice to the person struggling right now because they need cash: take the time and connect with people you find interesting. If you see something or someone you like on LinkedIn, like or comment and message them. It is free to give comments, especially ones that are meaningful. If I had to start from zero today, that's what I would do. I had to start from zero with my current firm almost five years ago; I understand the risks. Be wise and allow for enough time to build relationships and contacts. The last firm I owned, I worked another job that didn't pay much…$9.80/hr. It didn't take long before I could leave. I used the money to run marketing and take advantage of the recession; then, since others were cutting down on marketing costs, I used it to gain awareness. It worked; we placed an ad where the right people saw it at the right time and contacted us.

I hear the unconventional, "Oh, don't go all the way, you're not going to do it if, you know, you're working in another job." I think that's BS. If you're single and you have the time, yes. If you have family and you're a working family, it may be a little more difficult, but work on it. The pandemic tightened banking and the basic resources many are utilizing to survive. I'm an advocate for going all in, with some financial support, whether it's part-time or whether you've got to do something else. If you're part of a family unit, help from your partner may enable you to do it.

It's going to take time. Unless you come from a wealthy background, or you can quit and have the money to do so, or you've got the financial reserves, it's going to take twelve to eighteen months minimum, in my mind, for you to take the time to build your business right. The best advice I've heard lately, "Build the brand first, then go get your customers." You'll likely have to pay somebody to help do that.

People will argue and say, "You're crazy. It can't be done." It's my feeling that the words *it can't be done* are the launch codes to greatness. The digital transformation allows many to create digital companies and lower the cost of entry into business. Utilizing branding to differentiate your business online is a wise strategy. This is where having extra funds to brand well is important. Website builders such as Web.com allow for an inexpensive way to brand until you can build revenue to engage a proven branding agency. It is traditional advice to take early funds and reinvest in the business to best position your firm for growth. I see this advice not often followed because in real-time, the resources are often needed to support sustaining the business. In my case I went all in with branding. In the downturn of 2008 and '09 I advertised not to attract government customers but to focus on branding to secure vendors. This strengthened my base and gave me a strong offering when my marketing had to be precise. Those first eighteen months are critical for building momentum. Most people don't come from wealthy backgrounds and aren't able to get immediate access to large sums of money. Most have to seek capital. Real life will tell different stories for how easy access to resources is for you based on your demographics.

Caring Produces Revenue

When you care, you're going to care about your vendor; you're going to care about the customer, you're going to care about your employees. You're going to be caring because it's a byproduct of what you believe at your core; others will sense that. They're going to sense that you're a person who's not working just to get a one-off order. You'll be more likely to say, "I'm coming to you as a vendor, a partner, a customer; I want you for the long term. This isn't a short one-off buy. What do I have to do to help you see that and realize that?" It's not always going to be profitable at first, however.

Jesse Itzler wrote one of the anthems for the New York Knicks, "Go New York," in the middle of the 90s; he's now co-owner of the NBA's Atlanta Hawks. He got paid $5,000 for the song, but it cost him $4,800 to cut the track. He didn't care that he only made $200; they played his song. Like Jesse, you might not make much money upfront; you might even lose money. He was making the point: you're not always going to make money the way people think. It usually isn't, "Oh. I started a business. I'm immediately profitable." Although he probably made royalties on the song he created for the Knicks, it was what came after that opened doors for him.

You should be working to build momentum in your business. You can't always be thinking about profit, which is why if you're working, stay where you are and build your business slowly. If I was my younger self, and not an advocate for college, I would have gone to work at a warehouse or a sales job straight out of high school (everyone needs to learn sales), stacked the money for five years, taken it to a bank, and sought a loan using the money saved up as collateral. I believe that I would have been successful much faster by avoiding school.

Then I would only go back to school for something like an MBA, even then, but you don't need that now—this is a skills economy, and I'd see things that way going forward. If you don't have compassion, what's the point? If Artificial Intelligence (AI) and automation can do everything, and yet the industry is saying they need people who know the soft skills about emotion in AI, then why won't humans learn this if they're working to teach technology to mimic this asset?

As technology and AI improve routine tasks for certain staffed labor positions, soft skills will be more valued, and businesses will be wise to place a greater emphasis on interpersonal skills and communications. Having a deeper understanding of others, whether they're employees, clients, vendors, etc., will be at the core of their actions. AI and technology have their place in creating efficiencies for humanity. In my opinion, soft skills will only increase in value to better understand how to improve technology and user experiences in the generalities of business. What they want in these roles are people who understand people. A computer has yet to flawlessly show the emotional IQ that the neurodiverse can do with ease. AI may eclipse those who currently refuse to see its value. Then there is comfort in saying AI will replace those who cannot show a basic level of empathy and emotional intelligence for others. When these technology firms start acquiring talent that can build the tools with emotional awareness, it will be hard for some. I began to notice articles coming out around 2018 or 2019 that noted the skills needed in AI were empathy and soft skills, which I thought ironic.

It's great that many are understanding the value of tech as a career path and learning to code. From my vantage point, it seems the tech industry is saying, "No, we need people who can think on a human level because computers don't yet know how—they will eventually learn—but how do you teach a computer empathy?" Somebody has to be able to input and give all those data points.

Decision making based on compassion and goodwill makes for increased revenue. I took a loss on a significant order because we refused to change one piece of the item that would make the unit unsafe. That person in charge of the entire program went to another location. When they were in a spot to decide who got the new order, when all things were equal, I was considered and won one of the major orders. I secured another contract because our way of doing business was ultimately based on empathy and kindness. The value was much more than what I lost.

In the early 2000s, I worked for a supplier who had a very popular gaming systems account. The head buyer for this massive company was buying the touch screen glass that went inside the device at what they later told me was roughly one hundred times the cost of what I quoted him.

When I first quoted him, he asked me, “Are you sure that’s the price?”

I said, “Yes.” I could tell by his tone that something was off.

He asked, “Can you confirm?”

I said, “Considering the urgency of the project you are working on, I am most certain of this price and its accuracy.”

His tone prompted me to inquire more about his reservations. He mentioned that this didn’t make sense and asked me if I didn’t mind showing what our costs were to ensure he didn’t miss the mark as this was one of their largest projects. I put myself in his shoes, knowing his career was on the line, and sensed no ill will from him. I sent him our costs before mark up. When he saw my mark up, he said, “I will never buy from that company again. Only from you.” He asked me why I didn’t mark up to the range he initially mentioned was what he paid for the item. I proceeded to let him know that historical data didn't call for such an exorbitant mark up. He was grossly overpaying. He told me I could have gotten away with this. I let him know that wasn't who I was at my core. His position at this company was the highest executive; a billion-dollar firm gave me advice and told me to continue to do things the same way because it would bring me success. It's not the standard, even though he felt it should be.

The weight of his position and firm was invaluable to me once I left that firm. When we bid our first deal that allowed for professional references in lieu of actual company work performance, he provided a reference. They called him and later let me know they were beyond impressed how someone from that high up spoke so highly of me. His reference was enough for them to take us seriously, and we secured a deal.

He retired about fifteen years ago, but it was interesting that he provided such a wonderful reference for me. At each stage of my success, I would check in with him, and his demeanor was often, "I told you this would happen." It reconfirmed what he told me when we first connected: "If you keep doing this for life, you will be successful."

Toxic Individuals are Dead Weight

Toxic people are detrimental to a business even if they possess superior talent. They kill culture, and nobody wants to work with them. As noted in the book *Extreme Ownership,* there are no bad teams, there are only bad leaders. Those in leadership positions can and should inspire and improve the overall success of those around them. This takes leadership based on empathy. As the person at the top, you're the person with control. A good leader needs to get rid of toxic people. It takes cognitive empathy to do so.

Extreme Ownership nailed this concept perfectly. It's not easy to say or do the tough things necessary to get the job done despite how others are feeling. Navy SEALS prepare hours in advance and build teams so that there is trust and proficiency when the time comes to execute a plan. My takeaway from this book is that empathy in business is the way to go. It takes an empathetic person to live and do things the right way.

Extreme Ownership gives an example of how one guy was complaining, "Oh, my team's bad, my team's bad." Hence, they switched him to be the leader of the best team they had; the other leader was given the complainer's original team. It didn't really improve the situation for the guy who was complaining. The other leader managed to get his new team to the front. That leader took a team up from the bottom, and he won—that team went to second and then first, and the team that the other guy led dropped from being first all the way to the bottom. This example shows that it's not the team, it's the leader. Leadership has the biggest impact when empathy is shown.

Toxic individuals are a cancer to teams and best removed quickly. It is showing compassion to other team members when doing this so as not to allow for a culture of negativity.

The better vendors take notice of the cultures of your firm. They may become aware of the tolerance of this type of toxic culture and remove themselves from working with you. The prudent ones may ask, "Hey, what's going on? This doesn't match your culture, this doesn't match the executives, this doesn't match customer service, this doesn't match all the follow-up and tech support, you have someone in here doing this? Why are you all allowing this?"

It ultimately reflects back on the leader. Many are quick to go on social media and say things about this type of negativity, and if not, they are certainly talking amongst themselves about it. Toxic individuals seek to spew all the negativity that can. They attack employees, they attack vendors, they attack customers, they kill dreams and ideas.

When do you walk away from a toxic situation or individual? What are some red flag indicators that you should not do business with these types of people? Some examples include situations where they pick up the phone and use profanity or racially discriminate against others. That's different than if somebody is just picking up the phone, having a bad day. In those situations, empathy may soften the encounter. People may respond well to you genuinely inquiring, "How are you doing? What's going on?" If someone is calling people names, or calling women inappropriate names, then there is a blatant intent to harm others and cause issues.

An initial red flag should go up if a person is off to a bad start and several interactions later show a pattern of unacceptable behavior. You'll begin to realize when someone isn't just having a bad day. Some people have an ill intent. If the teams you get passed off to from such an individual also exhibit the same type of behavior, I recommend you walk away. If top leadership is like this and supports this type of interaction, then it is usually a sign of there being deeper issues. In my experience, many felt comfortable telling me where I didn't belong. Those who made assumption about my capabilities showed their weakness, all to my advantage.

Sometimes it's just one person who acts inappropriately. In that case, hang up the phone and work to speak with someone else within the same company. If two or three different people exhibit the same behavior, they're basically telling you how their company works and who they are. You don't want to deal with them. You may not want to judge a company on the basis of one person's actions, however. If you've made contact with two or three touchpoints in the company and they all act alike, walk away.

If an executive acts one way, and you check their social media and see profanity and inappropriate things on their site, that's a red flag. Do your research—find out who you are really dealing with.

People love putting themselves out there; my advice is to check out social media, see what their position is, and what they support. Analyze what you see. Who are they showing themselves to be on Facebook, Instagram, and Twitter? If your social media presence doesn't align with what I already know about you, when I place a call with you, I am already attuned to the possibility of deception.

If you say, "Yeah, I hate playing golf," and all I see on your social media are posts about golf, I'm reassessing the ability for you to tell the truth. I am saying to myself, "OK, well, why are you telling me you hate golf? What's going on? Why does this person feel the need to lie to build a connection?"

That's why I said it's important to be a quiet warrior; do your research and then let them talk; they're going to tell on themselves. There should never be what's called a cold call; that's an old person's mentality. Your mindset should view every call as a chance to have a conversation. That sets a different tone and energy. There should be enough readily available information about the firm and an individual's role within it to start a conversation. Many business professionals use LinkedIn, and it's a great place to see if you have something in common and can align with them to spark a conversation.

When you engage with others, it needs to be heartfelt. Your vibrational energy shared in tones and body cues will prove to them how genuine you really are. When you ask how someone is really doing and mean it, they will be more likely to pick up on the authenticity in your voice. Use the pause and silence method to allow for them to respond. Listening shows you are engaging; your responses will most likely open a way to ask more questions. The knowledge you gain will begin to help with your application of cognitive empathy. Your replies, made with compassionate empathy, may provide them with the help they need.

Most of what you will gain in helping others is based on cognitive empathy. Effective execution in emotional and compassionate empathy will help cross into the end zone. It's like football. Emotional empathy is special teams returning the kick. The offense comes on and utilizes cognitive empathy to get downfield and into scoring position. Compassionate empathy is the red zone in which the offense can score the touchdown.

Large firms have red-line suppliers who are quick to claim that only they can support these firms. You may have a better chance of developing a win-win with these firms through an indirect approach. This comes from building a grassroots foundation by doing what they are most likely *not* doing as a large firm, and that is consistently showing empathy in all they do. Grow your firm to the point where you can bring a deal to them. There are certain customers to secure the pathway to winning via collaboration. It is an effective way to grow. Empathy in actions will help build these collaborations that will allow smaller firms to compete with those who are larger.

When you approach customers or vendors via the leverage of collaboration, you may run into those with full-blown attitudes. They may feel no benefit from working with you, so you might need to help them understand. You could say, "We have identified some gaps we fill well, and you could benefit as a contributing teaming partner. We are seeking to give you this opportunity. It may not work in your favor going at this alone on this specific deal. We are working to help you."

It's like the parable where the king pardoned a very large debt from an individual, and then found out that that person didn't forgive the minor debt someone else owed him. The king then put that person in jail for the original debt owed. That's essentially where we're at. We've had collaborative deals where the main source has given us full-blown flak and attitude, and when it became known to the "king," it then went really bad for the middle man.

In some cases, when the middle man lost the deal, we were able to bring in a new person who might have told us no a year prior, and they were able to take that spot. That's why it becomes important that when someone tells you no. Keep them in mind; the chance to collaborate with them might come back around and ultimately work in your favor.

Mind Mapping

Mind mapping is a technique that comes with practice. The easiest way to mind map someone is to assume a customer is a loved one and interact with care. How would you sell this product or service to a family member knowing you wanted the best for them? This framework will place you in the proper mindset to connect. Ask about them, ask what brings them joy about their work, and then listen. Or ask how can you help make their role easier. Then listen. Ask, then listen. Take notes. Then if you have questions, ask more inquiring "real" questions for understanding and stating your intent for wanting to understand.

You want to connect to a person's heart. You want to establish an intimate and authentic level of communication to address their issues with complete and compassionate solutions. This goes back to viewing the customer as a family member or a youth who is seeking wisdom. Be a funnel for enlightenment for them. The mind is a receiver; it takes what is being given to analyze to understand in the process. Slow down and speak from your core. The vibrations you share will be different, which will send a better transmission for the connection.

If you are nervous in sales, don't worry about it. Customers may sense your anxiety but will also realize your authenticity. They may reciprocate kindness to you as it typically comes across as seeking to understand, and you can ask them for their assistance in finding out what you want to know. If you tend to speak more than listen, force yourself to be calm and listen. This may help convey your energy and ultimately encourage a connection.

Three Types of Empathy

There are three types of empathy: cognitive, emotional, and compassionate. You need emotional empathy to feel what the other person is saying. There's mind mapping; what I'm referencing is how you move between each of those. If you meet a hard-nosed person that's just bang, bang, bang, you're not going to connect with them on an emotional level right away.

You're working to find out where their positioning is. The person who's coming at you hard, you really have a chance to win them over as a client, but what you have to do, you got to know how to move in and out. You need to know when to apply emotion to curb the intensity of an emotionally charged person showing high levels of negativity.

You've got to sense what is going on. You have to hear what is being said cognitively. You have to ask, "What's this person's issue? Let me work and understand it." Then you have to move between feeling and compassion. This is mind mapping. It's looking at who you're dealing with, the information you have, and how to use your mind, heart, and soul to deal with and apply to the situation at hand.

All these start with the tone and your reaction. It helps, when you first engage, to ask, "How are you doing this morning?" Your compassionate nature will be on display. Their response will give you a jumping off point as to how to interact effectively with them..

We are talking about interpersonal skills, and we are talking about empathy in a setting that a lot of people aren't familiar with, as this all relates to revenue growth, sustainment, and compassion. So how does mind mapping relate to revenue growth, sustainment, and compassion?

Emotional empathy. You are looking at the entire deal in the sense of the reverse profit, meaning you're still going to grow, but your profit's not going to be as high. For example, if you have a customer and your sales rep says, "Oh, this person is having a bad day, I'm afraid to tell them the price because of how they're feeling," they're not going to mark up the price the way they normally would.

Someone who is highly skilled in cognitive empathy will utilize emotional empathy to grasp the feeling of another and be able to mentally assess how to provide a solution that is beneficial to both based on wisdom and not just a feeling. Their interaction looks like this: "Your concerns are valid. From what I've heard you explain, and the conclusion we have come to, this represents value. This helps you." They're going to take into consideration how you feel; they're thinking how to best benefit you in the long run; they're providing value. They are being kind and not just nice, as previously noted earlier in the book. If you as the seller cognitively understand the situation, you're not going to seek to lower the price. And when you do that, everything you do is aimed at building a foundation.

Working to be successful in sales without empathy is like sending your team out to fail. And I'm not talking about empathy just for show. The idea of, "OK, fine, I'm going to get them later, I'm going to hook them, then do a bait and switch." No. I'm talking genuine empathy, and I think people will sense this; they're looking for you to be true to who you are.

Your brand needs to reflect who you really are. If it doesn't, you're going to get called out on this. Social media's going to call you out, and the generation of youth coming up have got real guts when it comes to exposing impostors. They will call you, or anybody, out because they fail to care about the things that are important to our current society.

Using the Mind Mapping Methodology

You've got to basically look at the other person and not think of yourself. If you're an employee inside a company, review the mission, review your company's purpose, and see what it aligns with. I think companies are changing where their purpose is going, and if they're not, they should be, because that's where society as a whole is going.

I'm talking about purpose. As a charity, or if your company's doing charity, your actions can start telling your purpose now. If your company is not current supporting worthy causes, it may be wise to consider how to get them involved for helping others. Success can be obtained while generating profits and making impact for those less fortunate. Leadership positions need to start thinking about all this now to stay in business.

Tips and Tricks

To train to use the mind mapping method practically, practice with some tips and tricks on employing the mind mapping strategy in real-time in the business world. This is all related to revenue growth, sustainment, and compassion. This is a practical use of the three domains of empathy that you need to execute.

Those high in cognitive empathy grow revenue *and* increase profits. In contrast, emotional empathy helps to continue the connection. It creates and nurtures a funnel for getting information on how to utilize cognitive empathy in action to deliver results with compassionate empathy. All three are needed, and how they are deployed will take time to master. This is best suited to move quickly from the person who is learning to show true genuine care. In short, be human, and this will tune your senses into understanding how and when to utilize this. It requires active listening; if you cannot "feel" the other person, hear deeply what they are saying and deliver the information back with kindness.

Slow down your delivery and mirror back the questions to show understanding, such as, "What I hear you telling me is such and such," or, "From what we have discussed, the takeaways lead me to understand you are looking for x, y, and z. So, how may we help you reach that point?" Continue asking questions to ensure your understanding is on par with their needs.

Now, how does mind mapping help you fulfill your goal of business success through compassion? It is key to showing the other person that you heard and understood them. It is your opportunity to show cognitive empathy from how well you connected emotionally with them. Suppose they are grossly incorrect in what they thought they needed or were looking for, and you have listened and can now provide the correct information. In that case, compassion allows you to deliver it to them in such a kind way that they not only leave you more educated, they feel human and connected that you said it in a way that doesn't belittle them.

For example, I was at a customer site with a vendor during a trade show. They wanted to meet the vendor that was with me. When we all met on the spot, the head person in charge of IT stated an issue and kindly asked how the vendor would solve it because there was an immediate opportunity. The vendor replied in short order, "The way you buy is old and stupid, and any person in IT knows this." The air in the space went flat, and the facial expression of the IT executive was in disbelief and embarrassment. I quickly stepped in and mentioned to the vendor that the process for this customer was a little different from the work they normally do, but the vendor kept going on until they could see the point that I was making, but the damage was done.

After the trade show, I went back to the customer and discussed that we had found another vendor who had a solution that fit and mirrored the kindness we both wanted to work with. That vendor was able to secure the deal, even though they initially weren't the top preference. The winning vendor's attitude and demeanor were worth the slight trade-offs for the few bells and whistles provided by the less kind and empathetic vendor.

The best step for you, the reader, to implement the mind mapping methodology is to listen. First, listen, take an active ear, be silent. If this is new, write down what you are hearing them say. When they pause, stop and acknowledge, and at best, let them work to get to their point across before stating back to them what you hear them saying. Think of how they may be feeling for their issue coming to you, and simply be a good human.

Kindness is a strength; empathy is what the greats do well. You have to know people and be curious about them to take your vision to full execution. If they ask for information and you don't know the answer, say you don't know, and you will work to find it. If you know the answer, offer to take time to get a good response back to them. Give a brief overview of what you believe them to be saying and asking for and take a team approach to your response. Say, "What we have discussed and we can do to help, we will respond… It is my understanding that these may be what you are looking for…."

It is usually the one in the room who is listening who gains the most knowledge. The wise are known for being able to hear and understand. This is the theory is behind the quiet warrior. This is the mindset of "attacking" the heart to understand. You assess concerns, feelings, and joys and how to tackle them with kindness, empathy, and compassion. It's listening as if your life depended on it because someone is giving you their time to express a concern. You are gaining information when you actively listen that will help you make them better for sharing or allow you to make a difference for their live or businesses.

Technology is shortening our physical engagement time with people. You must take care to let people see you *actually* care, and that this isn't something you are doing just to gain a sale. If you aren't genuine, then they will sense this and move on. Listening to them and letting them speak gives them control and allows them to be heard.

How do you turn a no into a yes through the mind mapping method? A no usually means that you haven't identified the issue or there is a timing flaw. The best way then is to help them think outside the current situation, meaning you address their no and then take the facts they gave and start removing or addressing them one by one so that they are down to the issue itself; no reasons are left and you can identify and address their concern. If you are told no, kindly ask if they'll share the reason why. If they persist on saying no, then give them three reasons they may not be aware of which describes why their industry would benefit from whatever you are offering, and then ask them if they want to hear more about it.

These are the ways to make connections between revenue growth and compassion. Make sure you build a foundation to grow on. Do not forget that for a new business, selling value is the important shift going on now. Always show value; to do this, you have to listen to the people you are working to help. You have to hear them and understand, and that takes seeing the situation from their standpoint, which requires empathy.

CHAPTER 5

THE SALES TEAM DOUBLE TAKE

The Big Sales Lie

There are many big lies about success, and one of the biggest is the lie about sales. Deception in marketing has created an environment where salespeople are often forced to bend truths to make sales. There are many opportunities to correct what was vaguely or falsely stated in marketing. Instead of taking the moral action and correcting these errors, many sales teams continue pointing fingers back at marketing. Customers do not benefit from this. In doing this, it creates a big sales lie.

Sales teams may focus more on making sales due to misleading information given to customers by marketing. These sales lie in the gap between truth in marketing and information given by sales. Neither side takes ownership, and this has to stop. The answer, in my view, is to adjust who has the hammer to correct this issue in real-time, and that is the sales teams. If incorrect information is given, there is an opportunity in the sales process to utilize cognitive and compassionate empathy to correct errors.

Ignoring the misguided information known by or made aware to sales teams during engagement to close a sale is a big lie. Sales managers often push their teams to continue closing sales and avoiding known issues in order to give the customers what is needed. With a disregard for truly delivering customer needs with a high level of cognitive empathy, these managers push their people to sell at the customer's expense. Compassionate empathy is overlooked, and disregard for emotional empathy shows a low proficiency in cognitive empathy to sell in this manner.

Engaging in sales with no consideration for what the customer really needs breaks trust. It can be seen as concealment of the truth, and brand strength suffers. It is a trying task to identify revenue teams that can deliver in this environment because companies are looking for the traditional sales professional. Companies would be wise to change their approach and look more towards those who can show empathy in actions. Sales leaders in many firms are not trained to properly lead teams in an empathetic manner. Sales systems are not set up to focus on the desire to understand the customer. I have seen firms set up pre-sales and then pass them on to a sales team member for closing. Trust is built in discovery. By omission in training and hiring, I feel sales teams lie to themselves and their customers by pushing hard for sales. American filmmaker Ava DuVernay said, "Be passionate and move forward with gusto every single hour of every single day until you reach your goal." I like to replace the word passionate with compassionate or empathetic.

Overlooking the importance of building relationships and taking the long-term method for growing revenue can be fatal when sales teams follow bosses who push hard selling over relationship building. Lying to a sales team working to build long-term relationship puts them in the position of unknowingly building relationships on false premises. These types of leaders are essentially lying to themselves, their teams, and most importantly, their customers. True leaders simply don't take this approach. This builds a relationship on a false premise, and such actions typically place teams in positions to do things that are not in a customer's best interest.

Sales Versus Customer Service

This is the ideal new age sales team. I have a deep appreciation for the quote from the prominent billionaire Mario Gabelli, "I hire PHDs: poor, hungry, and driven." The mentality is to forget your background. Are you hungry, humble, and driven? If you are poor in the sense that you want to make a better life, and the driven part is there in your mind, then you'd likely make a natural sales person.

The humble part fuses the other two characteristics into a successful individual. This three-pronged approach was how the military moved forward a few years ago. They no longer wanted just a quality product at a low price. They wanted a quality product that was delivered on time and within budget. You have to be hungry, humble, and driven to move forward and be successful.

I work to use the new age approach both with buyers and end users. I say, "Hey, look, tell me what you need and when you need it." Then I work with a vendor and say, "I understand these aren't your normal circumstances. Will you consider working with us on price and schedule because of what is important?"

I often work to convey my purpose to the vendor. "Look, I'm not working just to make the sale, okay?

If you can help us make this mission, which is about helping the end user, this is what we need: I need it here, or we'd like to have it there, so I can continue with my mission and purpose of being great in this space." But I also know I'm going to weigh the cost of how much I can take the hit to get it done or how low I can operate to get it done because, ultimately, it's about caring for the people at the end of the spectrum all along the way.

I come first from a position of ingrained empathy; I make sales based on that standpoint. I'm selling or positioning a product based on the likelihood that customers will have to call for support. And when they say, "I was sold this, it's not doing X," I'm selling from the point of issue X. I identify that if you're most likely going to have this issue with your product or service, that's where I'm going, "Look, here's the issue you're having. This product's great at this, but it's bad at this—we can make an improvement here. If you take it in your current situation, you're most likely going to have these issues. So, customer support is available. Here are the people that can help. If you have any issues, here's what you do."

When they call customer support, it's not a new issue. They're told of the potential cons on the front end. I'm selling a product from the point of knowing that there's a potential to have to deal with technical support or issues. In logistics, they say you're putting out fires all day anyway, so I start from where I anticipate the fire to be. As Wayne Gretzky said, "I skate to where the puck is going to be, not where it has been." You sell with the anticipation that if your customer winds up with an issue, what you're selling is the very thing to help their solution.

Hard Selling Loses Money

It is my deep belief that you help customers buy; you don't sell them. When I say selling, I mean hard selling without empathy. It is a complete disregard for the customer and their needs and only to benefit your quotas and goals. Revenue is my view of what comes from implementing empathy at the foundation of every relationship. Revenue is sustainable; selling is not. Selling to me has a negative connotation to it. It is from a mindset of forcing a customer to change and do what you want by deception. Building a relationship and offering value by cognitive empathy because the overall solutions benefit the customer relationship is revenue to me. It is a byproduct of the actions of empathy.

Merriam-Webster defines revenue as those incomes produced by a given source. The source, I would argue, is empathetic actions that yield income. Sales are the exchange of the commodity. Getting to the exchange without empathy is hard selling. It's seeking to exchange without developing a relationship. By this, I mean hard selling and completely ignoring the customer's concerns and issues. Revenue is how a firm operates. Hard selling, in my experience, is not sustainable.

I do not like hard sales, and am immediately turned off when approached in a hard sales manner. In most cases, I have already identified the competitor when a deal comes to the table and when the vendor's sales team pushes me hard. I say no, and in many cases seek to understand why they feel the need to push hard so I can help educate them for the next time on how to deal. I feel negatively about the brand because I wonder if the entire brand operates this way. I am sure others will disagree with my view on this, but this is my experience of what I have seen work, and not just with our supply chain partners three levels down, but with almost all our customers. Revenue comes from the sustainable business that builds a firm; these are your long-term customers and the acceleration of quality deals. Sales in these instances are short-term wins that are built on trust and lead to significant revenue deals. In our industry, you are usually tested on the smaller deals before the big ones come your way. How you act on the small deals is typically how you will on the larger ones when all things are equal.

Revenue Has Put Sales in a Time-out

Focusing on long-term revenue grounds the empathetic actions of a business. It provides time to build deep connections. This is similar to watching Usain Bolt in a race. I've often heard commentators speak on how he is slow out the gate, but his momentum and how he ended races were unmatched. He always had the end in mind. Building long-term revenue with empathy may feel like it is slow out the gate. It is actually gaining momentum, and the strides taken as the "race" progresses will mean your overall revenue will be based on how well your team and firm have provided actions to build trust with your customers for the future. Momentum is gained when a sales team gives free advice or products out of genuine care and authenticity. They are making deposits into the long-term revenue bank. When you help a vendor secure a connection that helps them grow, this is a long-term revenue deposit. These are authentic actions.

What is the best way to understand the difference between overall business revenue and direct profit from sales? Look at it like this: if you're only focused on the direct profit from sales, your customers will eventually be dissatisfied. They're going to find out you lied; you didn't tell the truth, then they will say, "I'm never buying from you again." And they will tell everyone else not to buy from you. Now you'll need to get five sales to replace the one sale that left. You missed out on the chance you were given to earn a customer's trust and empathy. As opposed to the revenue side, you build your base on genuine empathy and work to do the right thing. People will come knocking at your door; you're going to have revenue and growth because your mentality was never about selling first,it was based on your truly caring to help get the right thing done.

I have prioritized sales to align with my character. If you don't show signs of good character in knowing how to be kind and deal with people, then there's no point in talking. Prioritizing care and concern is what is at the forefront.

If you look at the traditional sales process funnel chart, the sale is not prioritized; the relationship is heavily at the forefront. Sales move to the last place. I'm saying to invert the process, flip it over, take the tip of the iceberg, stick it underwater, and everything above the water needs to be the primary thing you're focusing on.

I always approach people asking, "How can I help you?" For example, if you are selling hammers, nuts, and bolts, I would approach customers by saying, "Here's where I'm doing it. Have you ever worked with this customer?" And if they say no, "Would you be interested? Sometimes I do have another customer or a vendor that I use; I would like to use them and help you." The next thing that usually comes out of their mouth is, "We deal with such and such, such and such; we've had the most difficult time getting there, can you help?" My answer is always, "Yes, I can help."

I'm always looking for a position that isn't about the sale. I want to know how I can help someone drive their line into the customers that I have, versus a new person who's going to walk in there and just say, "Look, I want your best pricing, I don't want the sale if I'm not going to get the best price. I'm not going to use you if you don't get my price here."

Advisors often tell me, "Paul, you need to get a better price. That's not good." Well, I built a relationship; the better price will eventually come in the long run. "Paul, you need to get a better price, nail them down, get more money, more money, more money." Well, that's not what I'm doing. I've got a relationship going. Over time, I will make more money and have a greater positive impact by taking this approach. It has been said to me: "Paul, you're one of the kinder guys to come in and actually work and build a relationship and not tell us what we're going to do. We are one of the sole makers, for example, of the product or have our set distributors, but because you were this way, we're going to work with you and help you out. Thank you for giving us other business."

Our competitors walk in saying, "No, we have the contacts; you're going to do what we say." I'm going in there saying because they wanted to work with you, "How else can I help further that down the line?" It's all about building a relationship. Build the relationship, build the relationship, build the relationship…and then sell. People will tell you during this process what's needed to gain their trust. They are going to identify a window at some point, and you're going to ask, once you get past the initial part of them thinking you're not there just to make a sale, about the sale. You haven't made the sale yet—you're talking— I would say somewhere past the third or fourth time you talk, you make the sale.

When they start to see how you engage as a person, you then say, "Hey, look, when have you figured this time works?" This is the best time, in my opinion; when they can trust you, stating your opinion for a timeframe to do it, they will then reciprocate, telling you, "All right, I'm ready to do it here."

Knowing when the time is right is a gut feeling. Suppose you see somebody with a situation where they need to fill an order in the next week. In that case, you're pushing for urgency from an empathetic point of view. You're going to have to use a three-pronged approach of drive, purpose, and urgency.

The key that sales leaders need to focus on when instructing their teams is they have to care. They're going to have to show signs that they really care about the customer and their situation. They need to be able to listen. When you let people talk, they're going to tell you what you want to know.

Sales managers and teams need to live what they preach. Empathy, kindness, a genuine interest in your customer, and a belief in what you're selling are all important. Many salespeople think that this approach doesn't work; I know that it does. The problem is that most salespeople have not seen this approach in action, and it's not going to work if you don't believe it. If you're selling stuff you know is not good for the customer, it's not going to work. Sales have to align with purpose. When sales align with purpose, they're going to get behind it. They're all on one mission, to do the right thing and get it done. That's the biggest takeaway from this book.

It's sad, but most C-suite priorities are opposed to the fundamentals of business success built on compassion. Why? Because they don't think it works; they're bottom line people. There seems to be a push for change now that absolute power is in a position to be absolutely positive and leave a good mark. The old narrative is changing in a good way.

Individuals in charge should build a team around them that mirror the way they think. If you can get others to buy into the process of empathetic selling, that way of doing business will become infectious.

What I'm saying is you can't surround yourself with yes people. Empathetic people will have the heart to tell you, "That's a bad decision, and here's why."

CHAPTER 6

BENEVOLENT STRATEGIC PLANNING

Kindness and compassion can work for strategic planning just as it does in sales or any other area of business. We seek partners that strengthen our brand's mission and align with our goals, and in this way, we develop partners that know our stance, and our partnerships are very strong as a result. When people get to know the moral premise for which we are based, they want to build and keep a relationship with us. According to a 2018 research study titled, *"I feel your pain": A critical review of organizational research on empathy*, by Malissa A. Clark, Melissa M. Robertson, and Stephen Young, "The importance of empathy in the workplace has also been highlighted by recent popular press articles centered on developing and managing empathy at work, and organizational practices aimed at increasing employee empathy."

As an example, it was reported in 2016 that Ford engineers use an empathy belly when designing cars. This is a fake stomach you can wear to simulate how it feels to be pregnant while working to get in and out of a car. Apple's training manual, *The Genius Training Student Workbook*, is supposedly a comprehensive manual on how to empathize with people. The Apple manual, however, seems to be geared a bit more towards making a sale rather than genuinely working to help people.

I believe a business can effectively operate with compassion and kindness. It's a strategy that has worked well for me and others at very high levels. Looking at the roots of business transactions, they are between people. There is some element of compassion and kindness needed to collaborate or work together. It will solidify a brand when you show these actions. In addition, show other businesses that it is still possible to operate with kindness and compassion while still winning. A loyal supply chain can be created based on the premise of kindness and empathy.

How does being kind and showing compassion affect strategic planning? How do you do this and be successful? Let's say that you are looking to move to a new vendor. Vendors that typically fit well in assembling a solid supply chain or business align in purpose and mission. You're going to look for the vendor that aligns with your mission. I often ask, do they align with my values? And I do research on those people to make sure that they are authentic and true. For example, if I want to scale and use an outsourcing team for procurement, I usually will have consultants say to me, "Hey, we'll get our sales teams in here, and they can do the claiming for you." They're like, "What's the most important thing to you? Because we can close, we can close."

My response in those situations is that empathy is at the core of what we do. How does their product or service align with this? Do they treat their own teams this way? How do they handle difficult situations? What is their response? I make it very clear how important this is. My reputation is ultimately on the line with our clients when things don't go as planned. I am held to the standard of ensuring our vendors fall in line with the projects we support, and this is where the value is in what we do.

I am in the business of managing empathy at work and with our supply chain partners. I argue that most businesses are as well. The best doctors usually have the best bedside manner. They hear the root issue to the concerns of the patients. They show empathy and then correctly diagnose the situation. Sometimes they succeed in the resolution, other times not. However, those who felt the bedside manner may sense that they really care about them. The same can be said regarding business. Nothing is perfect, and how you make others feel can make a big difference. This is an elementary concept that works. It is an effective strategic plan that is best exemplified by the actions of the company's leadership and supporting executives. All others within the company can then align themselves with the purposeful mission.

One of the most important things in business is effectively showing kindness and empathy in actions. It is an effective strategy that has worked for me. It is authentically who I am. When I connect with others, I am also looking to see how I can help them outside of the needs I may have for the initial identification of them as a client or partner. I tell myself if I don't secure the deal, it may bother me. However, what can I do to add value to this person in showing kindness? I am looking to ensure this is a connection I can work with down the road. When I let them know to stay in contact with me, it is a genuine request, and follow-ups are planned, not just to check in to get new work. I follow up to see how they are doing in general.

Leaders most often ask me how can they live with empathy and not be seen as weak. I let them know that team members won't view them that way. They probably have team members who would appreciate a simple hello and a question of how their day is going. Some may have never been spoken to positively before. A leader has the sole power to live a life that can change an entire culture by the way they walk in their role. Those who see it as weakness are more fearful of the change they will need to make to live in a similar way. It's a good thing, and research supports that there is intrinsic value from seeing the imitation of empathy in action. Eventually, other managers will see it and adjust their behavior accordingly. Team members will typically adjust their interactions with others as well.

As an extension of your empathic way of life, your strategic planning needs to extend the same values and morals. If you have a vendor who does not, from the best of your knowledge, adhere to the same empathic principles—whether it's being eco-friendly or aligning to follow your same core values—then it's not a strategic move to partner with them. However, if there is an opportunity to show them a way to better affect their teams by interacting with you, it may be beneficial. This involves utilizing empathy to understand if it is possible. I have worked, in some situations, with a point of contact who was the top lead and who clearly didn't align with my values. In my moves to sever the contact during discovery, the questions asked about why they were in the role led to the real issue and the reason I saw that they needed kindness. In doing this, the person made a complete turnaround and led their firm with this lifestyle change. They later said they saw how it worked in action because of how I handled them at their worst moments. The root of their issue was that they didn't want the role that they had and felt that if they didn't keep up a tough persona, they would lose the respect and power they'd achieved after their parents had left them the firm.

When I heard this, I immediately understood that the situation required compassionate empathy; I put myself in their situation. I mentioned they were in a state of stress and living a life that might not best achieve their desire for respect. It was my recommendation that for twenty-one days they work on showing more kindness and empathy toward others. If it didn't work, put my advice in the same bucket as all the others they have received and count it as useless. If they began to see a slight change in response, the teams would be looking for authenticity to see how long they would continue this new behavior. By the start of the third twenty-one day period, they began to see a real change in how the teams responded to them. They saw this change, and soon their teams were showing a solid cohesiveness. They relayed back to me after eight months or so that the team members verbalized their thankfulness for these new actions. What was my reward? To see this change made. To see the positive results for deciding to engage a vendor who didn't necessarily fall in line with my values. It's not something I often do, and each instance is specific. It comes from working to understand another person and their issues. They became a good resource for us; I knew the quality and authenticity of the leadership. This example is proof that the best outcomes are usually from those who work on a long-term basis with authenticity in morality.

I recently engaged with investment bankers who are working for social change and a good cause: they make Personal Protective Equipment (PPE) from recycled materials. Their operation is based in the US, and their purpose is to provide a good product at a reasonable price, and then have the resulting funds go towards helping causes in the US and all around the globe. The cost of their product will be higher than their competitors. The PPE meets all requirements and certifications of the government. It struck a chord with me to see leadership living in a moral fashion that produced a product benefiting others around the globe. The push for helping the end user see this value is intense: it's important that customers know the purpose and reason for the higher cost of the product. People align with stories and purposeful causes like this. Empathy and kindness are being practiced, and others are benefiting from the company's mission. I have seen buyers pay top dollar to support companies when they feel they are backing the right cause. Your firm may not be in a position to buy from a company like this if saving money is the goal. There are ways, however, to help drive revenue to them by your recommendations or charitable support. This is also strategic in building relationships that might later help in your line of work.

How do I go about convincing people that it's worth doing the kind and right thing even if it's going to cost a little more? In the sense of what's going on in the world today, the task has become a little easier. If you asked me why I did certain things before COVID-19, they might have been difficult to explain. With everything that's going on, I feel like people are looking for a holistic approach and access to more B corporations. A corporation that is certified as a B corporation meets the highest verified standard when it comes to social, environmental, transparency, legal accountability, and profits with purpose. These companies are looking at the biggest challenges faced by society and doing something about them. They are stepping up and making inequality, poverty, the environment, and communities a priority and they use their profits to impact employees and the world at large.

Conversations are happening with investors who are seeking more socially aware companies. There is a big change going on now, so companies should accept the challenge and work to do good in their business practices. It will result in better outcomes for them and their customers in the long run. More people are becoming *aware*. They are willing to buy if you speak to their need for change. That change is obvious in actual brand advertising: you see words like 'eco-friendly, made from recyclable, we care about the Earth, social impact, climate, when you buy this money goes to help this cause.' Companies are putting information on their websites; they're putting it on their messaging; they're using it as part of their brand. They're actually identifying the causes that they're supporting.

We have all changed, in large part, due to the pandemic. In addition, you can look around and see big companies changing and reacting to a world that is now filled with social media and more accountability. In situations like the BP oil spill, the company needed to put a good face on their company and clean up the mess; now they are legitimately more environmentally proactive. Their strategic planning actually puts money and clout behind their social efforts. The Hartford's Future of Benefits 2021 study revealed roughly 75 percent of US employers provided more paid time off than federal and state-level mandates required. This same report also showed that 31 percent of employees fear taking time off will cause them to lose their job or be passed over for a promotion. Leadership has long overlooked internal and external strategic efforts based on empathy and kindness. The empathetic steps now being taken to create happier and more satisfied employees is a step in the right direction. Only time will tell, however, if these types of actions are authentic and indicative of true change.

If you look at it on a macro level, what is this generation after? They are coming into their own terms; they are growing up. They're basing decisions on social causes. You're going to have to consider what matters to them.

I mentioned an issue we had surrounding a vest order earlier in the book. The vests couldn't be deployed safely if the focus was on securing material that was a few cents cheaper. That wasn't the right thing to do, and it wasn't compassionate. You know you wanted to get the right stuff in there where the manufacturer's telling you, "Look, this is what needs to be done; it is the proper thing to do; don't cut corners." So, you go with the higher price for the vest and the window shield protection. You know that, ultimately, it's going to be a slightly higher cost, but in the end it was the right thing to do.

There's a honeycomb that goes inside an aircraft. Our vendor for the product mentioned to me, "Look, you can put this in there, it's just not certified." My response was, "Why am I going to put something in that's not certified? It's not the right stuff." They pushed back, saying, "Well, technically, the certification is coming; by the time the product has been delivered, it will be fine." I responded, "There are lives at stake. This is bigger than the price. I have family that served, and others are serving that don't know me. They depend on us to get their family home. It's not certified. Are you aware of what happens if something goes wrong? What happens if they use it now?"

We went with the higher-priced material to ensure safety. Being asked to overlook something to earn more money, in this case, was not worth it morally. There really isn't a price for someone's life. If something goes wrong, I would rather this material not be the cause for the issue. I went with a higher priced and certified sheet of honeycomb. It did its job and the material is still operational today and quite challenging to fight against.

It is a joy to be referenced by others as *growing* outside the box. It's the box of belief where most people think, "Hey, look, get it all, get it fast, get it now. Who cares? Get the sale from the person, then deal with it after." That just doesn't work for me. It's that old traditional model of "sell, sell, sell, sell, sell, and who cares if they don't need all the stuff you're selling them. Just sell it!"

It's unconventional for most people to look at things outside of the box. They're going to follow the status quo. What I'm saying here is that this new way of thinking will eventually become the status quo. That old box, that old belief most people have that you must be pushy and tough to win or be successful, especially at sales, is done. Engagement from the heart is what matters. Successful brands talk about the follow-up as being the success. Many people are not following up; their only concern is an immediate sale. If they do follow up, it is not based on empathy. Your approach needs to be consistent and intentional with value, and this can only be done with genuine kindness and empathy.

So, what are the best methods for people to grow outside of the box when strategic planning does not take compassion into account? Think unconventionally. Could someone from another domain in business who's clueless about your product see value in it? Get genuinely interested in another brand or cause and support them. Brands overthink themselves and what's in it for them. Get out and help someone else for no other reason than to help. It will pay off somewhere down the line. If it never does, you've done some good in this world.

An example of stepping back to see the entire picture while making long-term plans is a local business that wants to get more business. If they seek to set up their place as a disaster shelter to help their community, and really mean it, the community won't forget them. The long-term plan is what your business should be looking at. Who are you going to help in the process in addition to your customers? What is the premise for how you will get to your goal?

But, you ask, how will I know when a growth pattern has become outdated and must evolve? The discipline and passion behind your team is falling off. They have apparent signs of boredom and fatigue. You can see it if you look. The intensity of their work and team morale drops. Speaking frankly, this is something you should be able to gauge if you have been applying empathy in leadership and communication with your team as discussed in this book. Your team will give you feedback on how they feel and what they need. This result of leading with empathy will help you get ahead of any issues and make the changes necessary to evolve in alignment with your values and goals.

This seems so simple to follow, yet few are doing it. If you are not doing this, it is almost certain that your team is approaching an outdated growth pattern and needs to evolve. This is a different way to position your product. Evolving is a result of constant communication with your team and customers. You evolve when intel from your customers' buying patterns and habits change. This occurs best when you know them well and have a sense of care for them. Your customers will provide the feedback you need to help you evolve. In short, your customers dictate how you will evolve and grow. They will either tell you how you can continue to serve them or they'll go somewhere else. Your move is to know them well enough to be at the forefront of their evolution.

The Importance of Lifelines

That brings us to what I call lifelines. Lifelines are an important part of any long-term strategic growth and planning based on kindness and compassion. They are all about helping others. They are the actions being delivered; they are the message being sent out in your public branding. In short, lifelines are the long-term goodwill efforts that you're doing for no result other than doing and being good.

Somebody asked the question regarding how does a rural company get clientele? I responded by saying, "Why don't they turn their store into a disaster support center if something goes wrong? They'll have customers coming in for their immediate needs. For the long-term, they're letting people know if something happens, we're here for you." People will remember your efforts, and they'll come back to you. Similarly, corporations that align themselves with social causes or charities get that information out to potential customers. People who align with the same values will remember their efforts, and will come along with them as long-term customers.

The association with social causes and charities has to be based on a genuine desire to be empathetic and kind. You don't donate to charity thinking, "Oh, I'm going to make a million dollars off new customers tomorrow," or "I'm going to get that big contract." You do it to enact change. Eventually, people get wind that the company's intentions are genuine. You can't do one good thing and expect people to say, "Oh, this person or this company has credibility." You have to sustain your efforts over the long haul. Strategically, you're building social goodwill. In the end, you'll be rewarded for it monetarily.

Lifelines help people remember that you did something for them when you didn't need to. This could be a CEO at another company you're choosing to work with who happens to be a volunteer in your same social circle. You never know who supports which charities or causes; you might be surprised to find you've got a connection you didn't know you had. I wonder what the probability is for you to get a contact you need if you went out and found a random charity and started supporting them? Would you get a contact faster that way than if you just picked the phone up and dealt with them through the standard long sales cycle? You might cross paths with someone who's actually a decision maker in your field of business.

Strategically factoring goodwill and compassion into practice on a regular basis will help you develop relationships with people with similar missions. There may come a time when they need you, and you care about their mission because it's similar to yours, so you help them. Conversely, there may come a time when something happens, and you need them. Because of the relationship you've built, they will want to help you. They will literally act as a lifeline. They care about what happens to you and your business because they've seen you care about a similar mission.

There's another reason your strategic plan should include social goodwill. At some point, CEOs retire. While they may "officially" stop working, they frequently continue supporting charities and causes near and dear to their hearts. There are plenty of stories where individuals have had quiet patrons—former whales in terms of money and wealth—say, "I did not know that's what you needed. Here is money to help you because I've already seen what you are doing." You weren't really doing good to get money; you were authentically out there helping others. You need to be genuinely interested; your strategic plan needs to be focused on giving back because outside assistance or help for your business may not come. But who cares? What you're doing is giving back.

People can feel stagnant and as though they don't have a purpose. When that happens, they're not aligning to their initial reason for being in business. That's why your strategic plan needs to have social goodwill aspects to it. Employees may get bored with just everyday processes; change up the charity, the different things you're supporting, and ensure your team members align with these endeavors. That's when you say, "Look, these are the reasons why we have to keep going because these are the causes we're supporting." In doing that, people will realize that they need to keep pushing because there's something more significant going on than just working to make another sale.

When we realized that the supply chain needed to be updated and improved in this new COVID-19 world, we altered our patterns. We were already out there, wanting to help our veterans, but the pandemic took things to a whole new level. We reached out to the national supplier. It was a little easier in Austin because we already had access to a supply chain. We vetted people through our inner circle, and then they vetted their inner circle. It made it easier to keep our promises to our end users and lock in the supply chain. We dealt with that stagnant growth pattern by vetting the people through our trusted pipeline to speed things up. I reached out for a lifeline saying, "Hey, look, I know y'all normally supply this but do you have contacts in other areas in this field that you work with?" And because all of our supply lines cross, we got immediate access to vendors and other extensions.

Someone selling connectors and cables that had contacts in the medical field could help because they were already active in that same field. You never know who's talking to whom. There are inner circles of all types. With the military supplier, they had connections into the medical world and almost all different worlds, and we could quickly vet the whole supply line because of our lifelines. Build your lifelines strong and connect with everyone you can. In that way, your supply chain will be enormous and solid.

Audit Your Growth Patterns

There are many steps to properly audit your growth patterns. You can review customer engagements through surveys; you can pick up the phone and call a customer and seek nothing other than to say hi and appreciate them for being supportive of your firm. Match your story messaging to your care. When was the last time you got a call from Nike or Amazon to ask how your day was going and to say thank you for being a customer? The point is to use the technology and tools you have to monitor the time between buys, notes on why they bought in the first place, and what resonated with your firm that caused them to buy and continue to buy. Treat them as though they had been a customer for thirty years. Customer Relationship Management (CRM) tools help house a lot of data for tracking these data points. This provides you with the necessary information to follow up with customers.

My company has moved into the healthcare space and opened our lines for consulting with digital training. In doing this, we as a team have had to look at not only giving away what makes us excellent and losing the leverage of our primary line of business, but also ensure we don't tamper with the relationships we do have. Moving into this area is helping our team adjust to cross-selling in both the federal space and the healthcare space to provide our products as proficiently as we do for the government. It has driven our team to learn additional skills as well as open internal opportunities for them to work in a new line of business. We have refocused on solidifying our assets in one area, and focused new energy on growth in the healthcare and consulting area. We have become self-aware of how we can strategically grow our business while adhering to our original values of empathy and kindness.

How do you become self-aware so you can grow outside of the box? Self-help books are a great resource; they reinforce the idea that people will have to go through a learning experience to grow. I think COVID-19 was just such a learning experience for many people. Using empathy to place yourself in other people's shoes—to help you stop and listen to your client—can be your biggest learning experience. If you start from their viewpoint, it's a big step toward self-awareness.

Why are they buying? Why are they coming to you? What were the reasons that they chose to use your firm? You can start to assess all these things in conversation. Genuinely work to understand them. As noted in *How to Win Friends and Influence People*, Dale Carnegie didn't start off talking business to potential clients; he would first say something to the effect, "Well hey, how's the day going?" or, "Okay, I noticed you usually come down here and get a hot dog at this stand. Well, how was it today? What's going on?" And then, from there, by the fourth or fifth interaction, he's having a conversation. Well, this is what I do; this is how we can help. What can I do to help you further in this role? He never had an endgame, but he didn't start out of the gate pushing a sale because he was genuinely interested in others.

He wanted them to know that they could be seen and heard.

Find Your Why

Empathy and kindness is a mindset. Successful people take their goal and work backward. If you don't see your goal, what's the purpose of doing it? If you think, "I'm going to make this sale, I'm going to make this sale," well, why are you making the sale?

Coaching and self-improvement books frequently talk about finding your why. Successful people talk about, "Find your why, why, why." Well, you better know your goal for you to know your why. In *Think and Grow Rich*, it all starts from, "Why do you want to do it?" You can't just say, "I want a million dollars." Why do you want a million dollars? What are you going to do with it?

When you know your purpose for doing things, you're going to approach others from the proper perspective. You're not going to be thinking your interaction will only occur once; you're going to be thinking of your long-term alliance. Prior to working with PPE, our firm was just into military procurement. Prior to this opportunity, I didn't like dealing in the medical space. Suddenly, I could see, "Hey, look, this is something that's going on, there is no stockpile in the US for PPE." The willingness to grow outside the box enabled us to take a step back, assess the situation, and start supplying a product that could both grow our company and help others in the process. We now have contacts and suppliers that can help us do that. These are many new conversations that we're having with PPE, and we're setting ourselves up for long-term success. We're no longer pigeon-holed into just dealing with the government because we stepped back and said, "We need to address this sourcing for PPE."

During this process, I learned that one of our biggest advantages was we were able to vet people quickly. Originally, other people were selling counterfeit stuff; they weren't vetting their sources. We were able to do that quickly with our network based on benevolence. Our contacts were with people legitimately making things in the US for social cause reasons, like investors making US-made products out of recyclable products that can be vetted and traced. Now you are getting the right people in there who are vetting their supply chains because they ultimately know that the supply line had to be shored up—because at first, there was the mentality of, "Just make a sale, make a sale, make a sale." There have been tons of reports of people breaking laws and getting caught. They go to jail working to help only themselves, whereas if they really helped others, they would not be in trouble.

The traditional way of thinking, "I'm just going to make the sale and get rich" is not sustainable. The people who are left doing business now are those that are legitimate and authentic and kind in their entire approach for making their products. When the orders first came in, however, less reputable vendors sold counterfeit products that could not be used.

At that time, we had people making PPE stuff who had never done it before. They were working to do it for the right reasons, however. Now, those are the companies that are starting to stick around and secure products and long-term deals and getting vetted in the supply chain. Essentially, the people who had the long-term strategic plan within PPE to do the right thing weren't the ones who made all the money. The ones who were just about the bottom line and doing their thing made more money, but they aren't sticking around. Now that the world has shifted a little bit, there is a dire emphasis on PPE. Everyone's going back to the people that have been doing the right thing the whole time because they're the only trustworthy ones. They have risen to the top above the quick sale people.

Being adaptable, strategic, and driven with purpose is an excellent way to grow and prosper. Connection to others matters. The speed at which information moves gives an advantage to those who gain access to correct information. In my experience, the information needed to take quick action often comes from great relationships. It's the right connections that matter. Being strategic isn't often seen by others as the best path forward. The effective application of empathy and kindness is a path that is elusive and often catches the competition off guard.

Dealing With Change

It takes cognitive and compassionate empathy to have "buy-in" from your teams. You have to reassure them that what you're doing is not going to affect them negatively; they're still secure, you're not making them obsolete. It is a strength to position your company this way. It will require much reassurance on the front end. The right way to grow the firm is to say, "Look, this is the kind and right thing to do to grow this company."

When we first started getting other contracts and new people, some of the older employees started to feel like we were going to make them obsolete. I told them one by one, "Look, this is not what's happening; you were here first. We're going to work and grow so you can be in positions and attain that growth. But I am unable to move you up if we don't have the workload and the sustainability, or you're just going to be going to another job in the same role." They needed reassurance that those who were there prior would not lose out in position or place. You have to consider that they're worried and concerned that the company could fail, and they'd all be out of a job.

Always remember that there can be a lot of emotion around any kind of change. It is something many are simply not trained to deal with well. Cognitively, this needs to be addressed. Old ways are comfortable. Technology is advancing quickly. There needs to be a mentality of readiness. These changes are also high in cognitive costs: many are afraid of the sacrifices they might need to make and meet change with combative tactics. It requires you to meet their concerns with cognitive and compassionate empathy.

There are human costs to the pivots required to fill skill gaps; time to learn and adjust to new proficiencies is needed in order to succeed in the new line of work. Less time will be spent on the resources that are typically making the funds for the business. It would be wise to analyze the costs associated with the learning curve but not something to be looked at as the deciding factor. Presenting a pivot or change with facts and compassion towards the long-term benefits can be useful, especially in aligning team members to the new purpose.

Position any argument based on the team member leading the resistance. In some cases, this member is a cover for the ones with genuine concern. Look and listen to learn the truth. Team members are typically paid for 100 percent of their time. The efficiency of the work done usually gets better over time, as does the quality of the work. You can bring value to team members by creating space for them to think outside of the box for potential threats or pivots to keep in mind. When they address them, take it seriously and deploy up to a max of 25 percent of their time to it. It allows them a sense of purpose and contribution to their goals.

The cost for pivots is wasted time and resources for training current team members if a plan was not initially done correctly. What you want to analyze is the cost for time being spent on learning and working to grow the new lines. In short, if you have an employee or team that you are paying for 100 percent of their time and can proficiently run the primary line of business at 50 percent, you are essentially paying for 50 percent of the employee's output. Take 25-35 percent of that time and apply the resources to the new line since the business's current line only needs to operate at 50 percent to sustain itself. Eventually, if there is a success, the new line will be able to operate on 50 percent of the 25-35 percent given resources. To know that you are growing methodically, look at the long-term value of the pivot or growth.

You have to make sure you're leveraging a majority of their time. If someone's been in a position long enough, they have perfected it to where they're doing it at probably 50 percent of their capacity. So, the other 50 percent of that capacity could be used towards a growth pattern, something they're not used to. You've already sunk the cost in them being able to do their job efficiently.

Let them work researching this new area that is similar in scope at 25 percent of their time. You don't want to be engineering NASA projects then go over to baking cakes. You want to ensure that your new line is still in the same domain. You just have a different type of end user. Your team members will already be using the same level of brainpower and energy; let them use that additional capacity they have left over after they've perfected and become efficient within their current role on something new.

Google came out with the Innovation Time Out (ITO) policy to encourage employees to spend 80 percent of their time on core projects and the other 20 percent working on new ideas that interested them and helped channel their passion. This concept helps make a profit for the company with new ideas and products and keeps team members engaged and thriving.

Some positive effects that can happen for employees in a pivot include learning a new skill and becoming more confident in their abilities and association with the firm. You have given them "equity" and allowed them to bring value by assisting the firm in a new project. This is an intangible benefit that can never be taken away, especially if your endeavor is successful. Team members also gain experience during the process, which will be useful if you decide to pivot again. The outcome will be co-workers who align further with your purpose. On the flip side, if you fail, it is a learning experience. There are no failures if you learn from them. Even lack of success can be positive, whatever your outcome, because your team tried to do something new and learned from it in the process.

The entire team has to believe in leadership and purpose. If they are tied to the purpose when morale suffers, they will redirect to the purpose that is driving the business. If your mission and purpose are not clear, this becomes difficult because they will have difficulty focusing on reaching the goal. Motivation won't be enough if they can't align with the purpose. When your purpose is clear, it will override bad morale and allow them to get back on track. They will look at setbacks as obstacles to overcome to reach the purpose. The mindset is different. A moral compass matters because it will help align your purpose. It will set the guidelines for what your team will do to reach a goal.

Purpose should drive your business. A business should closely analyze whether its actions align with mission and purpose. The mindset for the encounters and opportunities presented to the business will then be clearer. Making pivots without thinking of the firm's purpose hurts the brand and could put the firm in a position to eradicate its initial purpose completely. A business in the process of change should ensure that the new long-term goals aren't in opposition to its original purpose. It may not be the best idea to pivot if it will cause your business to change its purpose and customer base completely. If the change enhances your mission and purpose and adds value to it, then it's worth pursuing. If you are aligned with your customers, your pivots and growth should also be in line with where they are headed as well.

Our firm added another revenue channel with a service-based offering. This added additional value for our customers. The cost to train new and current team members was high on the front end. It required more certifications, but implementation of the system will only make them better at their jobs and increase customer satisfaction. The buy-in from the team was easy because the new task fell in line with our original purpose to get our military personnel home safely. Our purpose and mission are ingrained in our actions. We do what we do because people depend on us. The mission and purpose overrode any feelings of not wanting to do it; we perceived the negative cost of not pursuing our new purpose as higher in the long run. You can lose everything if a pivot is not done correctly. But if the risk of not making a change is much greater for everyone involved, then it's a risk worth taking.

You might not know the effects of the pivot at first; that's why you should have a goal in mind. You should be focused on a short-term goal because a short-term benchmark will align more with your long-term strategic plan. You can't pivot long term and not deal with your short term because it can affect your current line of business.

Empathy is the driving force behind effective communication. Many reports now detail the high levels of stress for personal and company cultures that are not in tune with an empathetic leadership. Research supports empathy as a leadership trait. Connecting with others from a genuine place to feel, understand, and support them will allow you to better position yourself to build genuine connections and relationships. This matters in all businesses and especially when bringing your business into a global marketplace that already has local and regional competitors.

To compete where the mindsets are focused on cohesive and holistic principles by approaching business from an individual mindset may leave you on the outside without any chance for connecting at a deeper level that will help you grow. Look to show emotional empathy with customers or clients and truly listen to what they are saying. It will increase your level of success in applying cognitive empathy for relaying back to them with compassionate empathy what is being told to you. This may show that you're more inclined to fit the generalized mindset for collaboration to succeed in another country.

Success Based on Human Connection

Business has always been based on human connection. It is something that cannot be overlooked in your locality and certainly not when working to grow in another country. Show kindness in actions. Find a story or topic that genuinely resonates with you that you can inquire about from their side; they may have a backstory that you didn't know about.

Happy employees are beneficial to the success of a company. Profits are a derivative from engaged team members. Be curious about others; it places you in a mindset to show empathy to others. If an empathetic mindset is out of the norm for you or you feel it is not an innate characteristic, curiosity is a great place to start your journey. Showing compassion to others runs parallel to curiosity. They will feel a willingness that is genuine and authentic; the more it is practiced, the more it will become a habit. When gratitude and a thankful mind work together, it leads to a framework for compassionate empathy.

You have the power to be the change in your organization. Build your own methods for assessing your teams, look for the cues for things that seem "off," and listen to their tones during communication. Take time to listen more and speak less. Your efforts need to be authentic to be effective. Leadership should note the extensive research showing the value of empathy in their roles and how it flows down to all team members. To lead and not value excellent management who are showing themselves skilled in empathy is setting them up for failure and burnout.

Now, my intention is that you will see that kindness and compassion can work for long-term strategic planning, just as it does in sales and every other area of life. It's time for you to go out and look for partners that can strengthen your brand's mission. Make sure they align with your goals and know your stance, and your partnerships will be strong and productive. When people get to know the moral premise on which you are based, they will want to build and keep a relationship with you.

My reason for writing this book is to show others that success in business is possible while living a life of empathy and kindness. It would touch my heart if, a year from now, I were to hear how this book changed someone's life for the better after they made a commitment to show more empathy in business. That would bring me immense joy.

ACKNOWLEDGMENTS

There are so many people in my life who have been instrumental in building a foundation based on empathy in their actions towards me and for rearing me. There are those who are daily involved in my success, and who I am truly grateful for, as well as so many supporting people who have crossed paths with me that have left excellent learning experiences for me. Every interaction no matter how brief has led to my writing to express why I believe empathy is so critical in business and life. Before I thank so many others, I would first like to thank my wife Shana, who has been a pillar of support in my life and throughout building this business. Her behind the scenes actions to lean on have been extremely instrumental in the successful completion of this book.

Secondly, I am deeply grateful to my parents Paul Sr. and Donna—their support is beyond any written words for how indebted I am to how they've instilled living from a foundation based on empathy in my brother and I. During my most difficult times in business I was able to lean on their expert advice. Their encouragements assisted in helping me endure. I am truly blessed to have them as parents.

Third, to my brother Stephen, who has endured the deepest and toughest moments with me growing up and in our business ventures together. His unwavering support to give unfiltered advice and how close we are has meant everything to me. His services as a Marine and what has been done for our freedom is driving force for why I wake up every day knowing a family member like myself wants theirs home safely as well. I am truly thankful for having a brother like him.

To My mother-in-law Betty Lou, who has been an instrumental part of supporting me through this business and for giving invaluable support living with compassion in her actions to be a perfect example to inspire our growth. I am truly grateful for her.

To our son Logan, this was written as a way for you to see that kindness and empathy are a foundational block to grow in this life as a man. It is how Papa G and Dona raised Uncle Stephen and I. Never forget your greatest gift to this earth is how you live as an example to others and that your kindness echoes in eternity. You are able to succeed in great leaps when your foundation is built on this.

To our daughter (my stepdaughter) Melissa, this was also written as a way for you to see that you are equally capable as any man to accomplish all you desire in this life. Leverage your intellect with kindness and so much will be accomplished.

I would like to thank all the clients we have ever worked with that have made this even possible. They have been critical in proving that empathy is perfected when given and shown. I have been on the receiving end of so many clients that have done this for me. To our vendors who have done so much for us being able to support our clients, I am without words for their support and all they have done. Due to the nature of our work, I will not name them and many of them know who they are for all they have done.

I would also like to acknowledge retired Lt General Willie Williams, General Joaquin Mavalet, General Vincent Boles, General Ann Dunwoody, and to every single vendor, banker, and partner that has ever worked with us. There are particular ones who know who you are that have done so much for me personally and professionally because of the kindness you have shown. Others who have supported me in deserving of immense recognition and thanks are: Greg Walker, Justine Pogroske, Rene Godefroy, Nicky Dare, Jacqueline Way, Sanjoy Kuma Malik, Jyostsna Savant, Rathika, Rachel Mitchell, Mathews Tembo, Jesse Iwuji, Matt Casto, Leaderpress Team, Simon & Schuster's, Rachel Cook, David Mathis, John Jefferies, Michael Guiliano, Jeff Vettione, Gabe Thomas, Toni Smith, the Kaikini's, the Chatterjay's, the editors at Entreprenuer, Inc. and Forbes, BizPrenuer Middle East, Sohil and Eva Khan, Tej Brahmbhatt, Dr. Marina, Dr. Azzeza Jalaudeen, Lisa Miller, Quintin Nelson, Tara Nelson, Brandon Smith, Caroline Watson, the F1 Fupport Team, Anglin CPA, Shanee' Moret, Larry Yatch, Joy Sceizina, Olivia Joy Chavez- Caroll, Jacob Caroll, Red Team, C Team, L Team, M Team, Ghost Team, Blue Team, Black Team, N Team, Sibel Terhaar, and Brad Lea.

I want to also thank all those who paved a path for me and I want to acknowledge the following organizations making a difference in this world for others to learn about and support if they find value in their causes support their efforts:

idDareFoundation (www.nickydare.com) (https://idarecares.org/). The goal of iDARE's core programs are to raise awareness, educate, connect and engage supporters, empower leadership, and empower advocacy efforts.

365 Give (https://www.365give.ca/). 365give inspires people to create a better, happier you and a happier world by developing a daily giving habit—one person, one give, one day at a time.

Jesse Iwuji (https://www.jesseiwuji.com/). In all things Jesse Iwuji does, there are two constant elements: his devotion to service and his inspirational nature to many. Jesse went from competing at the top level of Division-1A college football to rising the ranks of the military as a Lieutenant Commander, and is now the only current driver in all of NASCAR at the national levels that actively serves his country as a US Military member.

A Kid Again (https://akidagain.org/). "Helping children build lifelong memories for families in your community who have a child living with a life-threatening condition."

MCHF (http://www.mchfzambia.org/). "Creating a path and hope for the underprivileged rural poor children and youth."

Brave Inspires Brave (https://www.braveinspiresbrave.com/). Heather McWilliam is a strong advocate for social justice, mental health, and human rights. After winning a landmark human rights case against the police while being an officer herself, Heather witnessed her BRAVE become the butterfly effect for countless others to step into their brave...

To all those unsung heroes, heroines and those I haven't named but who nonetheless have been pillars of support, inspiration, and guidance in building a network of success grounded in empathy, you have my limitless gratitude and respect in demonstrating to me personally how I can succeed the right way.

ABOUT THE AUTHOR

Paul L Gunn, Jr. has built his career around procurement, logistics, and supply chain and is a proven leader in business process management with an impressive track record evidenced by his firms' flawless delivery of performance records, including support to the DoD and Allies.

Paul has demonstrated his expertise in consulting, training and project management, implementing quality management systems, and deploying technology solutions for global organizations leading cross-functional teams in Asia, Europe, the Middle East, and America.

Paul Gunn takes an active role in all the firms he has owned including KUOG Corporation, leveraging his preferred servant leadership style and SME to drive all project phases from proposal generation to planning and execution, leading one of his firm's largest Quality Management System implementation projects for highly visible DoD end users. KUOG recently secured a max contract for $1.6 Billion to support the Air Force. Gunn credits empathy as a foundation for securing this supporting venture.

As founder of KUOG Corporation he led the firm to reach Inc's Fastest Growing Privately held firms at #273 in 2021, with his previous firm listing at #67 in 2014.

Mr. Gunn holds a Bachelor of Arts in Sociology from Georgia State University and a Master of Science in Business Administration from the University of Phoenix, and is a USA Today and WSJ Best Selling Author offering his results in consulting regularly on empathy in business. He is also a Founder of Watertusk Corporation.

Made in the USA
Columbia, SC
05 December 2021